HOW ☼ THINGS ☼ WORK

HOW FLYING MACHINES WORK

TERRY JENNINGS

Kingfisher Books

Kingfisher Books, Grisewood & Dempsey Ltd, Elsley House,
24-30 Great Titchfield Street, London W1P 7AD

First published in 1992 by Kingfisher Books
2 4 6 8 10 9 7 5 3 1
Copyright © Grisewood & Dempsey Ltd 1992

BRITISH LIBRARY CATALOGUING IN PUBLICATION DATA
A catalogue record for this book is available from
the British Library

ISBN 0 86272 925 4

Typeset in 3B2
Phototypeset by Southern Positives and Negatives (SPAN),
Lingfield, Surrey
Printed and bound in Hong Kong

Series editor: Jackie Gaff
Series designer: David West Children's Books
Author: Terry Jennings
Text contributors: Jackie Gaff, David Jefferis
Consultant: David Jefferis
Cover illustration: Micheal Fisher (Garden Studio)
Illustrators: Chris Forsey pp. 6-7, (insets 10-11), 12-13, 22-3,
(insets 26, 33 bot.); Hayward Art Group pp. 20-1, 24-5, 32-3,
34-5; Simon Tegg pp. 26-7, 36-7, 38-9; Ian Thompson pp. 2-3,
4-5, 8-9, 16-17; Grose Thurston Partnership pp. 14-15, 18-19,
28-9; Ross Watton (Garden Studio) pp. 10-11, 30-1.
Research: A.R. Blann

The publishers would like to thank: airship & balloon
Company; Britannia Airways; British Aerospace (Commercial
Aircraft) Ltd; Cameron Balloons Ltd; Counsel; Dowty
Aerospace Propellers; Ferranti International; G. Mottram;
GEC Plessey Avionics; Penny & Giles Data Recorders Ltd;
Rediffusion Simulation Ltd; Short Brothers PLC;
Sloane Helicopters Ltd; Thomas Sports Equipment Ltd;
Thunder & Colt Ltd.

CONTENTS

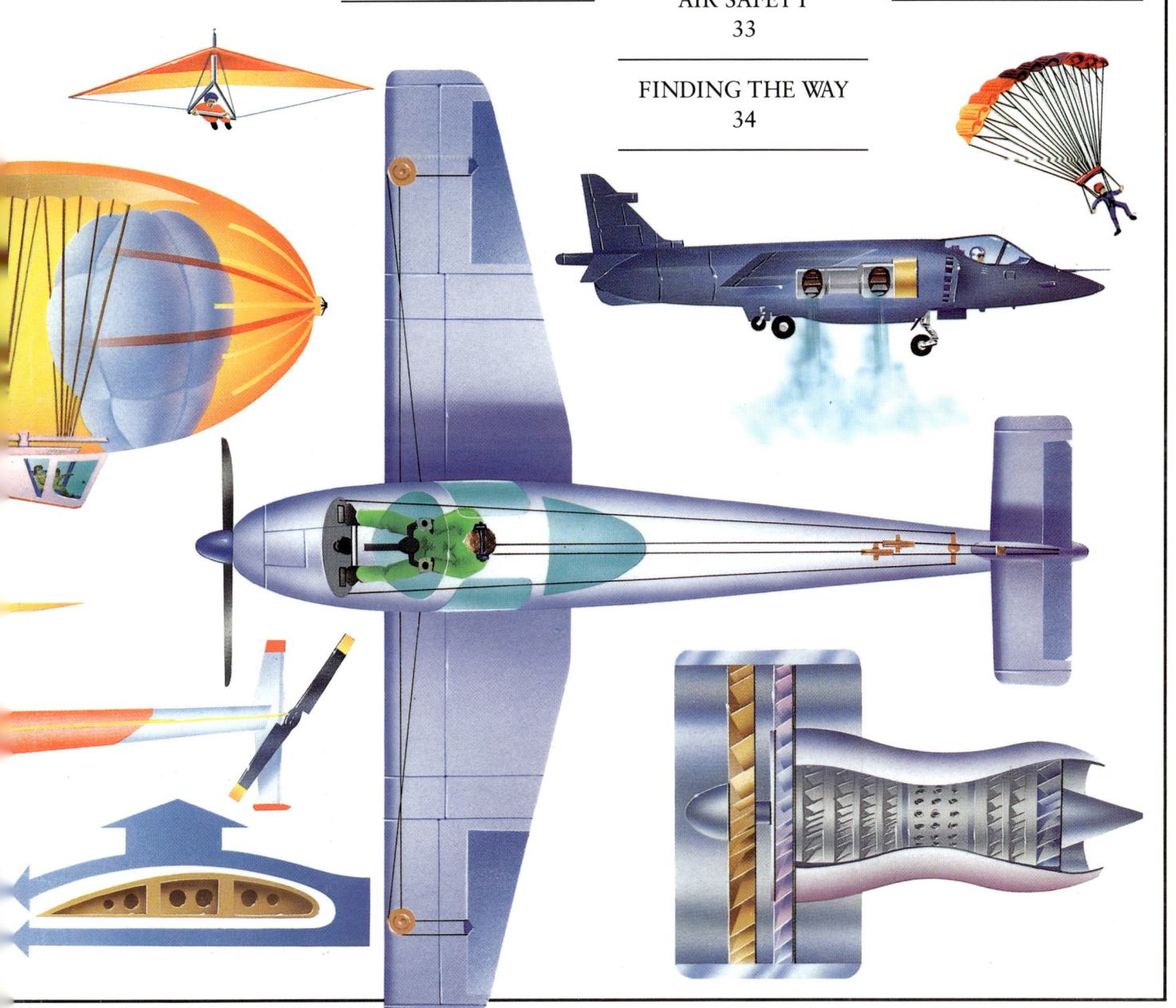

FAMOUS FLYING FIRSTS

▽ In 1783, in France, the brothers Joseph and Etienne Montgolfier launched the first successful hot-air balloon.

In 1797, the first safe parachute jump was made, by Frenchman André-Jacques Garnerin.

▽ In 1852 the first (steam-powered) airship was flown, by the French engineer Henri Giffard.

▽ In 1853, flight pioneer Sir George Cayley of Britain sent a man aloft in a monoplane glider.

▽ In the 1890s, the German engineer Otto Lilienthal built and flew hang-gliders.

△ On 17 December 1903, in North Carolina, USA, the first-ever powered aircraft flight took place. The aircraft, called *Flyer*, was built by Orville and Wilbur Wright.

△ In 1909, French pilot Louis Blériot made the first successful aeroplane flight across the English Channel.

△ In 1910 the first commercial air service was established, by Count Ferdinand von Zeppelin of Germany, using airships.

△ On 14-15 June 1919, two British pilots, John Alcock and Arthur Whitten Brown, made the first non-stop flight across the Atlantic.

▽ In May 1927, the US pilot Charles Lindbergh made history when he flew the Atlantic solo.

In June 1936, the maiden flight took place of the first practical helicopter, the German twin-rotor Focke-Achgelis Fa61.

In 1939, the world's first jet-propelled aircraft was built and flown by the Heinkel company of Germany. The He178 was a small single seater.

△ In October 1947, the USA's Bell X-1 rocket plane became the first supersonic aircraft.

▽ In May 1952, the four-engined de Havilland Comet became the world's first jet airliner to enter regular passenger service.

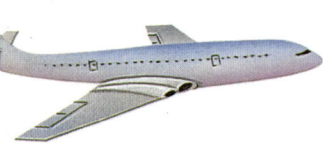

In May 1953, American pilot Jacqueline Cochran became the first woman to go supersonic.

△ On 2 March 1969, the Anglo-French Concorde made its maiden flight.

▽ The world's heaviest aircraft is the Russian Antonov 225, a six-turbofan freighter weighing 508 tonnes.

▽ The world's largest airliner is the USA's Boeing 747, or jumbo jet. It is over 70 metres long and the most recent models can carry over 400 passengers. Fully loaded, the giant plane weighs more than 400 tonnes.

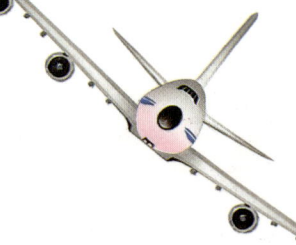

▽ The world's fastest aircraft is the USA's rocket-powered X-15. In 1967 it reached a record speed of Mach 6.72 (7297 km/h).

INTRODUCTION

A Greek myth written almost 3000 years ago tells of Icarus, who fell to his death when his wax and feather wings melted because he flew too high and too close to the heat of the Sun.

Less than 1000 years ago, an English monk broke both legs after testing a pair of wings by jumping from the tower of his abbey at Malmesbury.

Perhaps the most famous person to dream of flight was Leonardo da Vinci (1452-1519). This great Italian artist and inventor was fascinated by flight and sketched plans for all sorts of flying machines.

Leonardo's helicopter

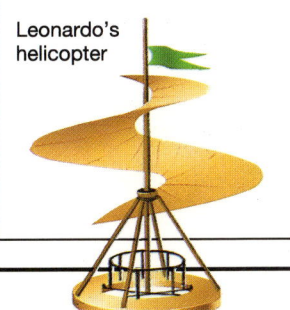

People's fascination with flight goes back to the earliest times. It is possible that even cave dwellers looked longingly at birds swooping through the air and wished that they too had wings. A few brave but foolhardy people tried launching themselves off cliffs and other high places with home-made wings strapped to their arms, but all of these early attempts to fly failed, some of them tragically.

It was only when people began to understand the power and properties of air that flying machines became possible. In fact, the first successful flying machine had little to do with the winged flight of a bird. Instead, it made use of a very simple principle – that hot air rises.

Since that discovery, just over 200 years ago, aircraft have progressed from the first slow uncontrollable balloons drifting in the breeze, to jets that are capable of travelling at two or even three times the speed of sound.

This book looks at the scientific principles that make it possible not only for aircraft to fly, but to travel farther and faster than people even a mere 40 years ago would have dreamed possible. After thousands of years of life at ground level, people have finally conquered the skies!

FOCUS ON HOT AIR

Hot air rises because air expands (spreads out) to take up more space when heated. The tiny molecules air is made of move apart, making the air lighter or less dense.

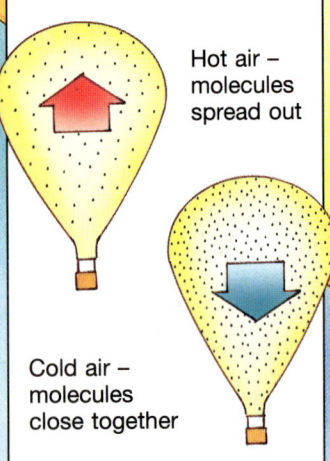

Hot air – molecules spread out

Cold air – molecules close together

As air cools down, it becomes heavier or more dense because the molecules pack closer together. This makes the air sink down again.

FLOATING ON AIR

A hot-air balloon is simply an enormous bag made of very light material which is filled with hot air. It floats in the sky because hot air rises, and hot air rises because it is lighter or less dense than cold air.

The bag of a hot-air balloon is called an envelope. It has to be big so that it can hold enough hot air to lift and carry the basket and the crew. The bigger the balloon, the more it can lift.

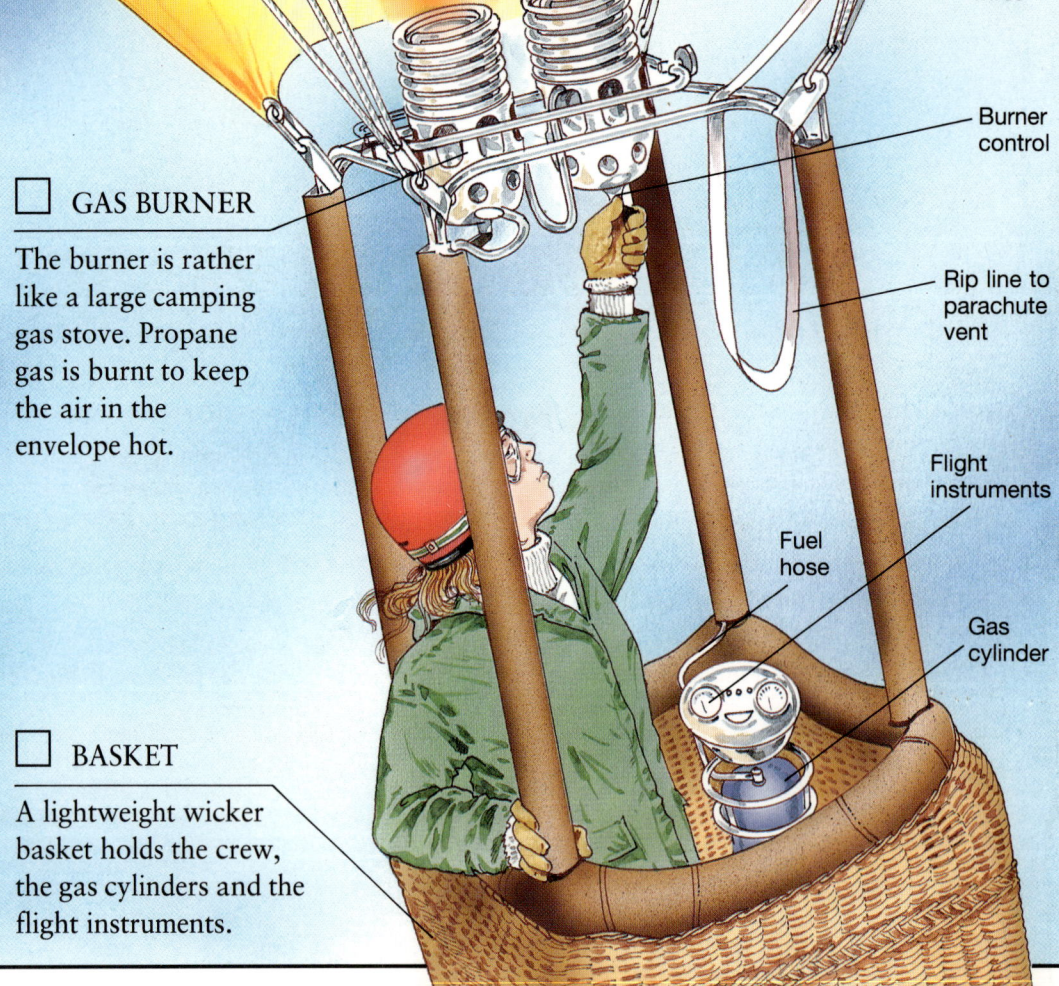

Rigging wires

Burner control

Rip line to parachute vent

Flight instruments

Fuel hose

Gas cylinder

☐ GAS BURNER

The burner is rather like a large camping gas stove. Propane gas is burnt to keep the air in the envelope hot.

☐ BASKET

A lightweight wicker basket holds the crew, the gas cylinders and the flight instruments.

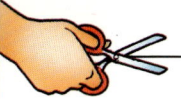

TEST IT OUT!

Here's a way to prove that air expands and takes up more space as it gets hotter. Fix a balloon over the top of a plastic bottle, then stand the bottle in hot water. The balloon will get larger and stand up as the air inside it and the bottle expands.

What happens if you now stand the bottle in a bowl of ice-cubes?

Balloon stands up

Bowl of hot water

 PARACHUTE VENT

If the crew want the balloon to come down, they can pull on the rip line to lower the parachute vent at the top of the envelope and let a little hot air out. Heavier cold air flows in to take the place of the hot air, adding weight to make the balloon come down.

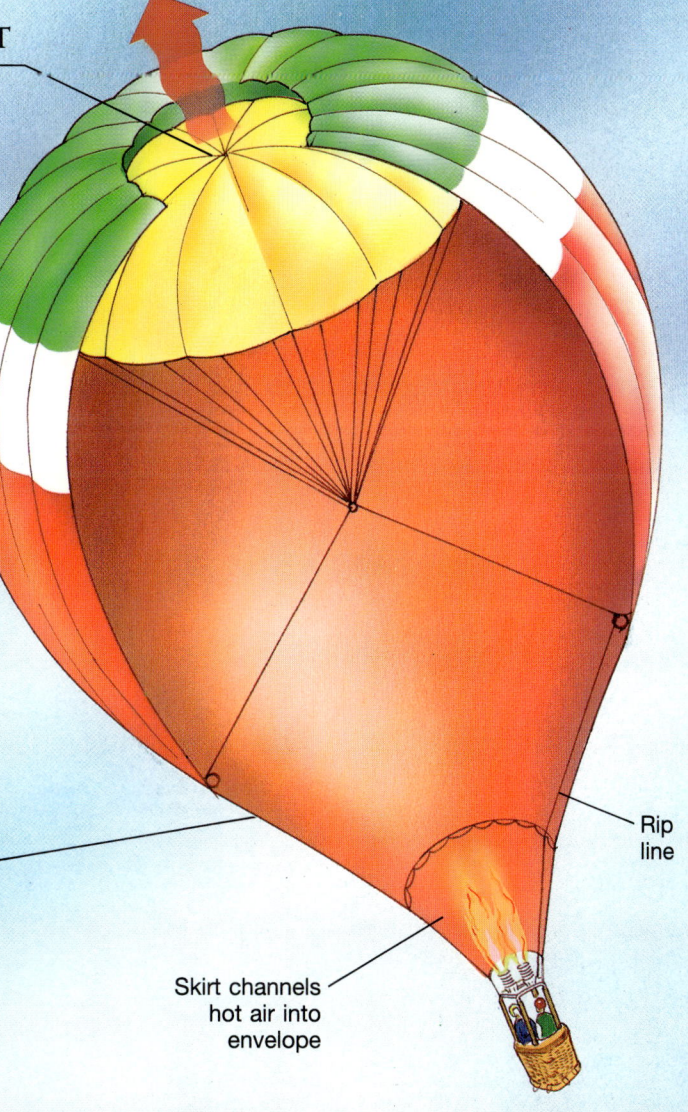

Rip line

ENVELOPE

The envelope is made of tough but light nylon. Hot air rises and pushes against the inside of the envelope, lifting the balloon into the air.

Skirt channels hot air into envelope

HOW BALLOONS FLY

The pilot can't control the direction of the balloon – it goes where the wind takes it. Its height depends on how long the pilot uses the burner for, and therefore how hot the air is inside the envelope.

Going up

To make the balloon rise, the pilot turns the burner on for quite long periods of time.

To keep at a steady height, the pilot turns the burner on for about 5 seconds, then coasts for about 20 seconds.

Coming down

To lose height, the pilot either stops using the burner for quite long periods, or opens the parachute vent a little to let out some hot air.

LIGHTER THAN AIR

There are gases that are lighter or less dense than air. This means that unlike air they don't need to be heated to help things fly. One of these lighter-than-air gases, helium, is used to fill the envelopes of modern airships.

Because air is heavier than helium, it is held in special bags called ballonets and used to control the airship's height. Pumping air into the ballonets, for example, adds weight to make the airship come down.

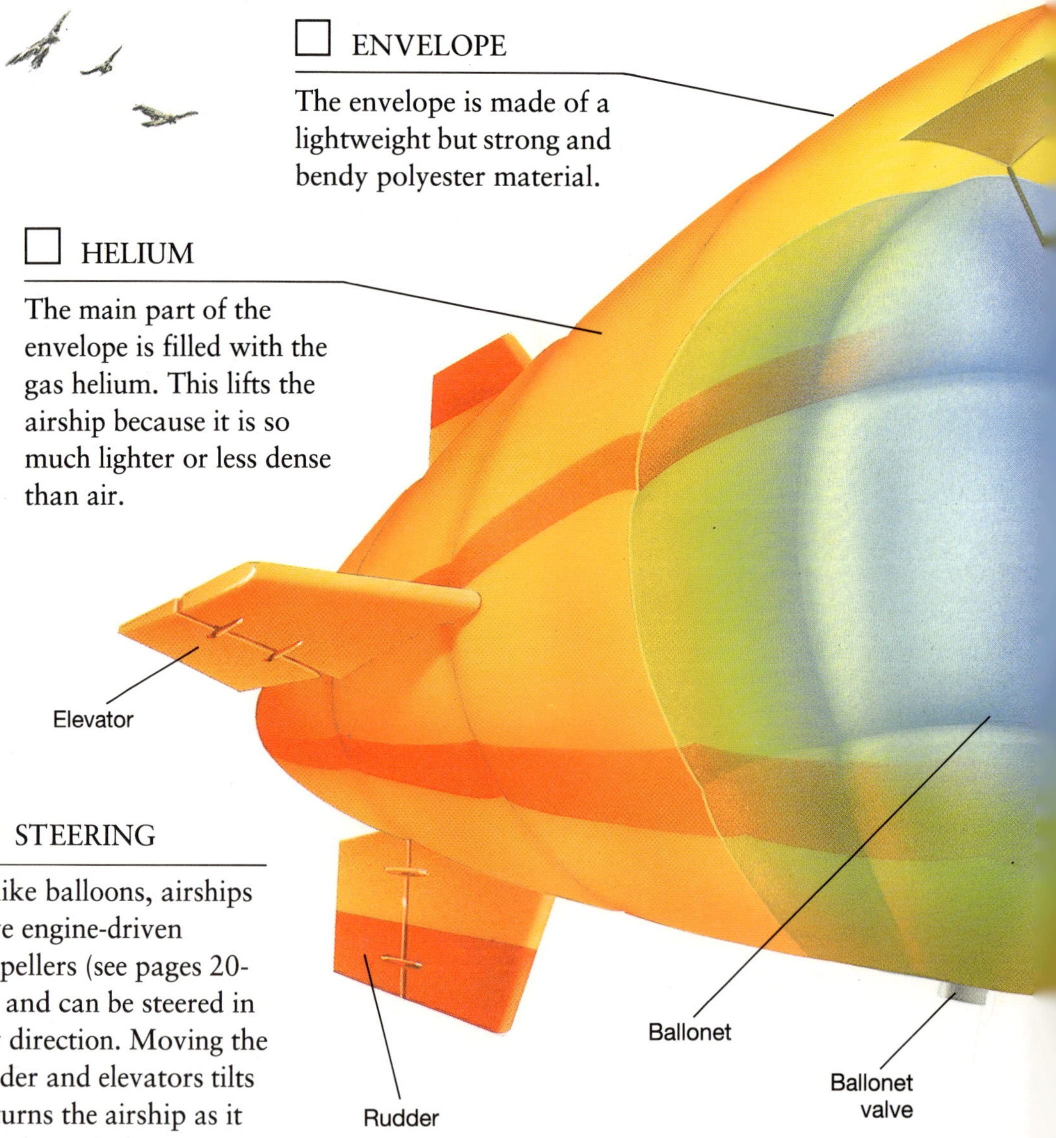

Air is a mixture of gases we can't see, smell or taste. The main gases are nitrogen and oxygen. But there are also small amounts of carbon dioxide gas and the gas water vapour, as well as traces of some rare gases, including helium. Air also contains tiny particles of salt, dust and dirt.

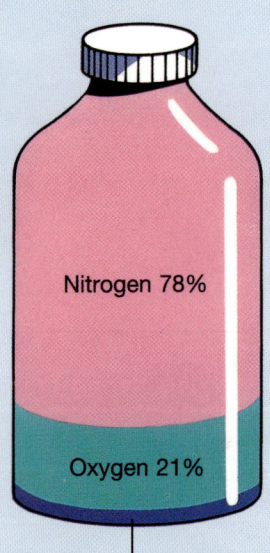

Nitrogen 78%

Oxygen 21%

Other gases 1%

Helium gas is about seven times lighter than air. As well as being used in airship envelopes, it is used in some types of fluorescent light tube and in some lasers.

It is obtained, not from air, but from wells that produce natural gas.

☐ ENVELOPE

The envelope is made of a lightweight but strong and bendy polyester material.

☐ HELIUM

The main part of the envelope is filled with the gas helium. This lifts the airship because it is so much lighter or less dense than air.

Elevator

☐ STEERING

Unlike balloons, airships have engine-driven propellers (see pages 20-21) and can be steered in any direction. Moving the rudder and elevators tilts or turns the airship as it flies through the air (see pages 14-15).

Rudder

Ballonet

Ballonet valve

☐ HOW AIRSHIPS FLY

When air is pumped out of the ballonets, the airship is light enough for the helium gas in the envelope to lift it up into the sky.

To make the airship heavier and bring it down, air is pumped into the ballonets by the engines.

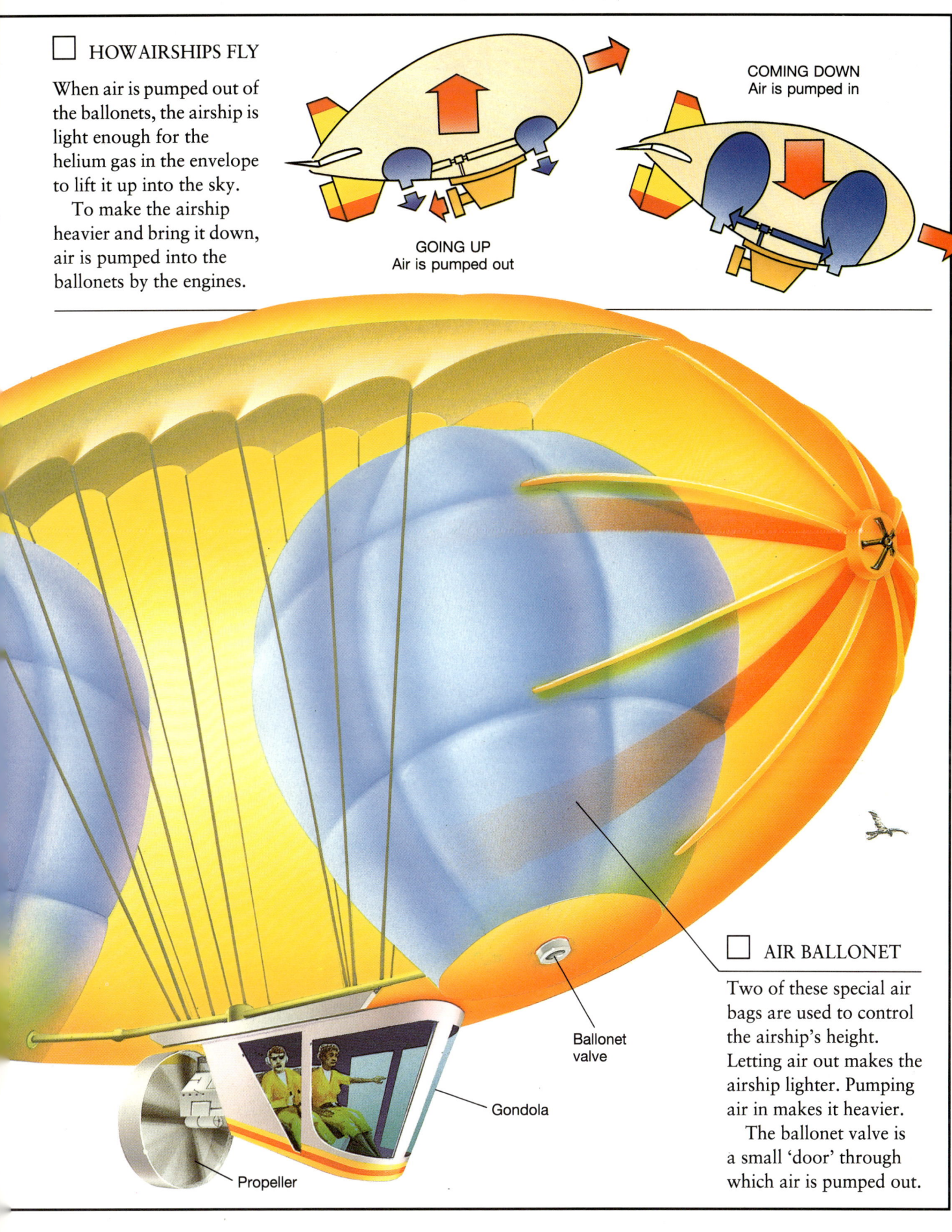

GOING UP
Air is pumped out

COMING DOWN
Air is pumped in

☐ AIR BALLONET

Two of these special air bags are used to control the airship's height. Letting air out makes the airship lighter. Pumping air in makes it heavier.

The ballonet valve is a small 'door' through which air is pumped out.

Ballonet valve

Gondola

Propeller

WINGS, AEROFOILS & LIFT

Hot-air balloons and airships can fly because they are lighter than air. But most aircraft are heavier than air and can fly only because they have wings. Wings have a special shape called an aerofoil, which is curved more above than below. Aerofoils are important to flight because an upwards force called lift is created by the way air flows around them. Winged aircraft can fly only when there is enough lift to overcome their weight, and when they are moving fast enough to create lift by keeping air flowing past their wings.

Did you know that if you were to draw a square with sides of 1 cm by 1 cm, the amount of air pressing on it would weigh 1 kg! Air is pressing on everything on Earth all the time – so much so that it has weight. We call this weight air pressure.

The Swiss scientist Daniel Bernoulli, above (1700-1782), discovered that as a liquid or a gas travels faster, its pressure decreases (lowers).

☐ AIR FLOW

Air flows faster above a wing or aerofoil than below. This is because the curved upper surface of an aerofoil is longer (from leading to trailing edge) than its lower surface. The air flowing over the aerofoil has to travel farther than the air flowing below, and it has to speed up to keep up.

☐ WING STRUCTURE

Aircraft wings aren't solid. A thin 'skin' of lightweight material covers aerofoil-shaped ribs supported by girder-shaped spars. This makes wings strong, but as light as possible.

Direction of flight

AIR FLOW

AIR FLOW

Leading edge is rounded

TEST IT OUT!

Hold a piece of thin paper just under your lips, then blow hard over it. The paper will lift! The air you blew over the paper moved faster and had less pressure than the air under it. This difference in pressure created lift.

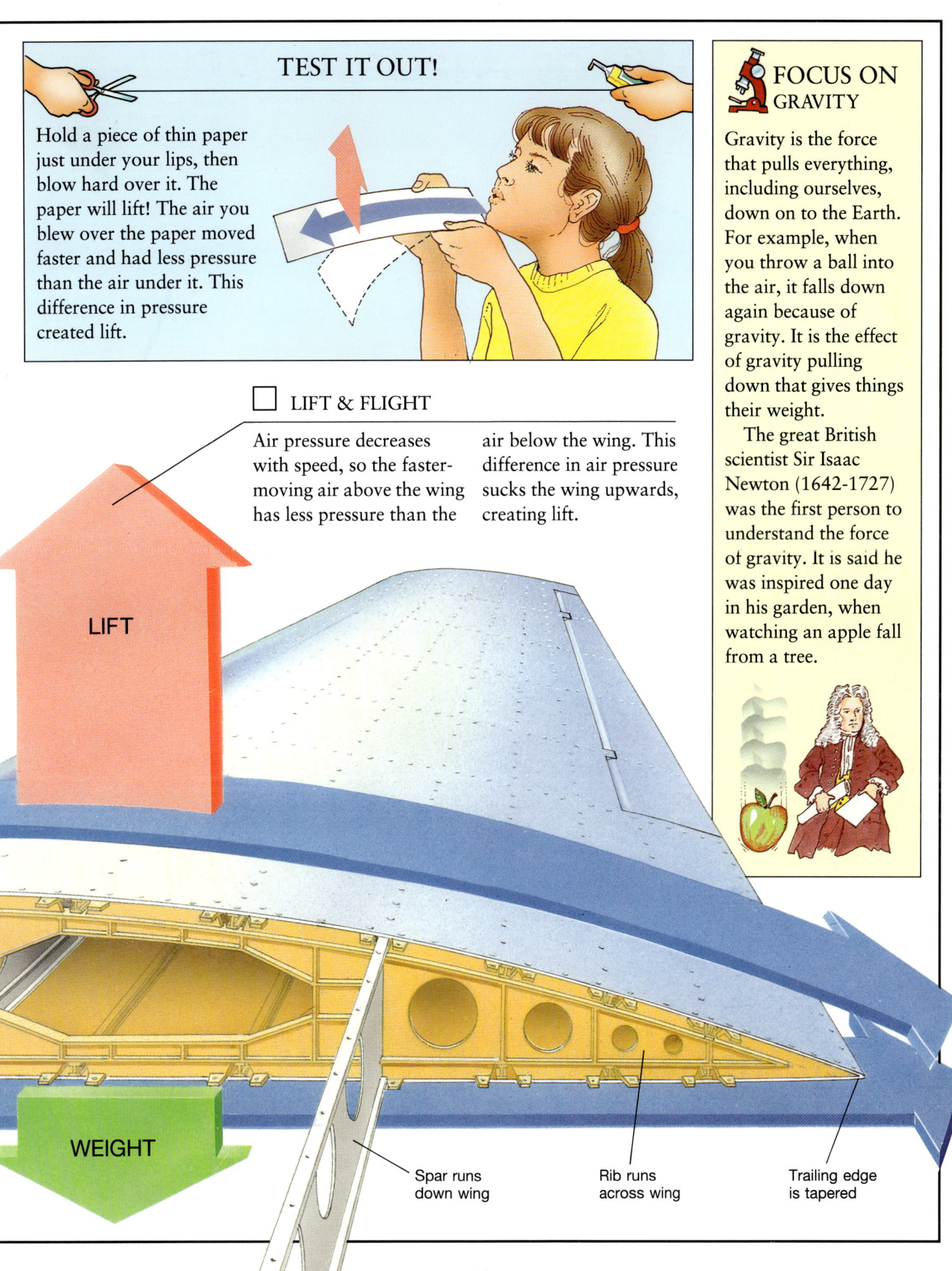

LIFT & FLIGHT

Air pressure decreases with speed, so the faster-moving air above the wing has less pressure than the air below the wing. This difference in air pressure sucks the wing upwards, creating lift.

LIFT

WEIGHT

Spar runs down wing

Rib runs across wing

Trailing edge is tapered

Gravity is the force that pulls everything, including ourselves, down on to the Earth. For example, when you throw a ball into the air, it falls down again because of gravity. It is the effect of gravity pulling down that gives things their weight.

The great British scientist Sir Isaac Newton (1642-1727) was the first person to understand the force of gravity. It is said he was inspired one day in his garden, when watching an apple fall from a tree.

Unpowered Flight

Most aircraft have engines to propel them along so that air flows over their wings, giving them lift. But gliders and hang-gliders don't have engines. Gliders can only be made to fly if they are towed into the air. Hang-gliders have to be launched from a high place such as a hilltop or a cliff.

Once gliders and hang-gliders are airborne, they keep air flowing over their wings by gliding slowly downwards at a very gentle angle.

☐ GETTING UP

Gliders are usually launched on a rope attached to a winch or a powered aircraft. The rope is released when the glider is high enough.

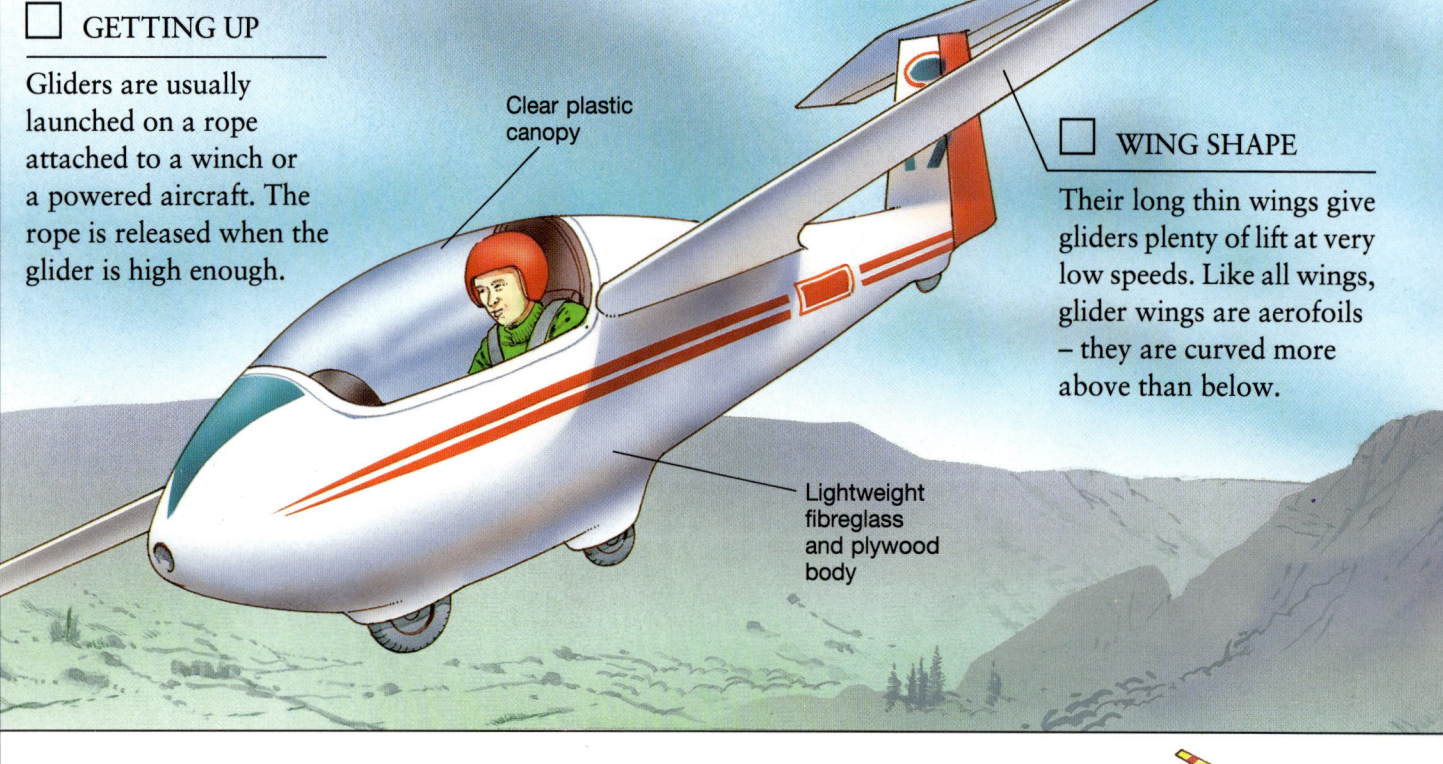

Clear plastic canopy

Lightweight fibreglass and plywood body

☐ WING SHAPE

Their long thin wings give gliders plenty of lift at very low speeds. Like all wings, glider wings are aerofoils – they are curved more above than below.

☐ HOW GLIDERS & HANG-GLIDERS FLY

Gliders and hang-gliders are so light that they can gain height by spiralling upwards in thermals.

Upward air currents also form where air is forced up by the slope of a hill or mountain.

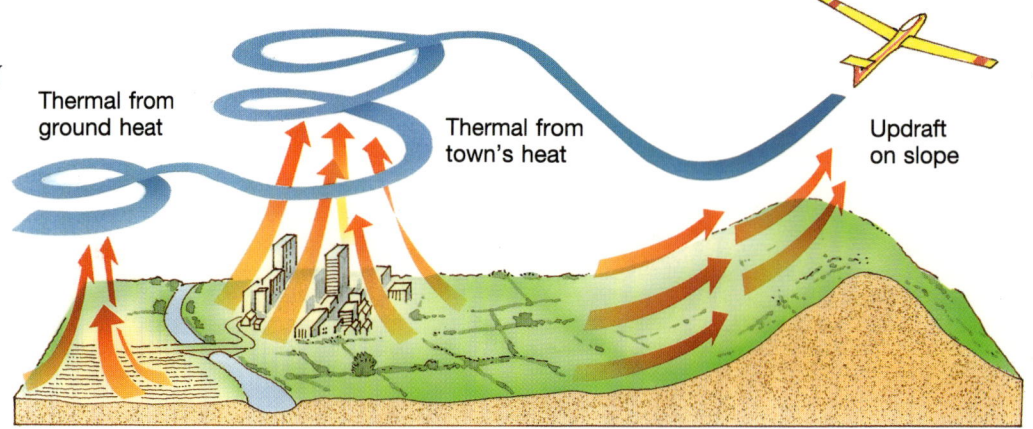

Thermal from ground heat

Thermal from town's heat

Updraft on slope

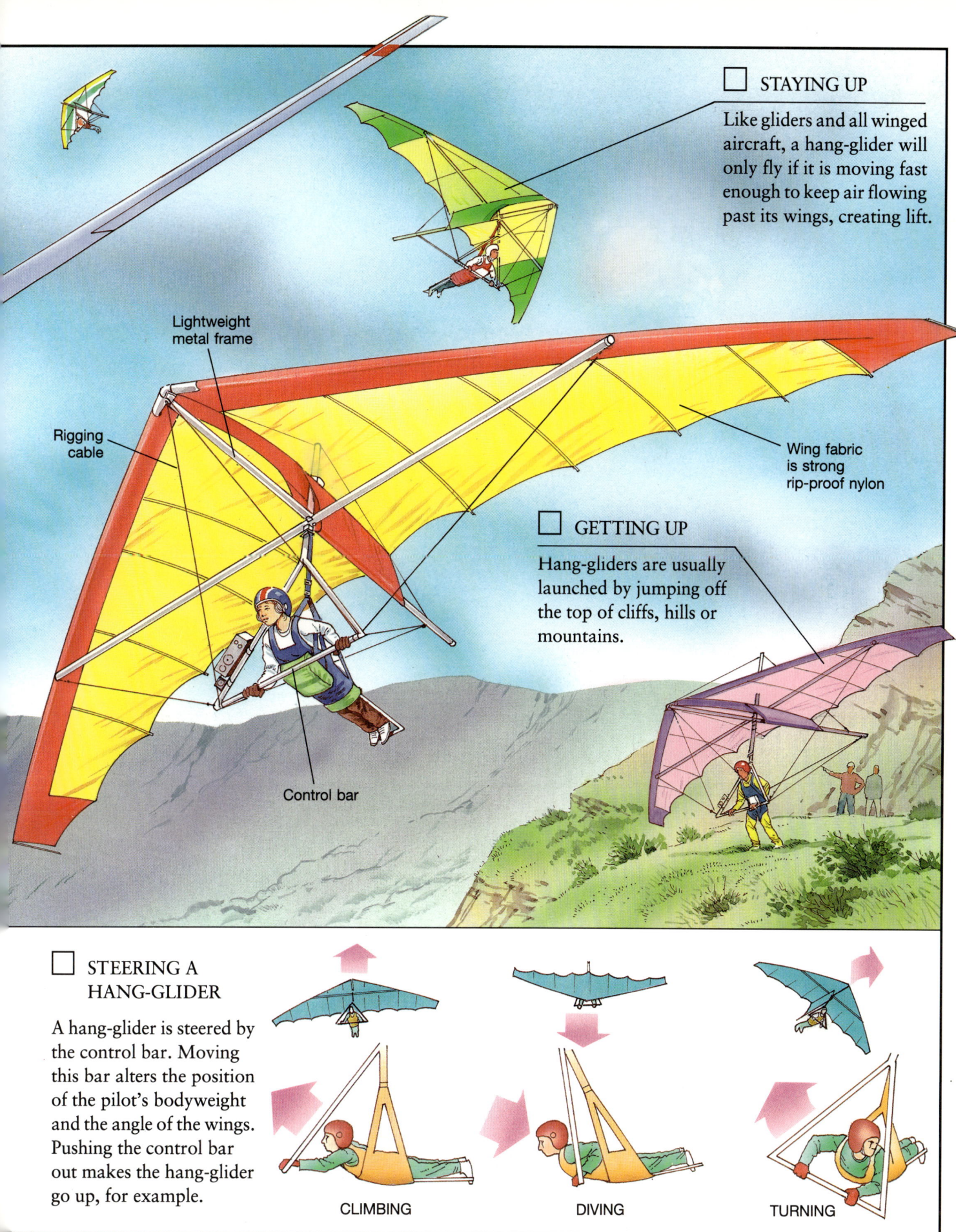

☐ STAYING UP

Like gliders and all winged aircraft, a hang-glider will only fly if it is moving fast enough to keep air flowing past its wings, creating lift.

Lightweight metal frame

Rigging cable

Wing fabric is strong rip-proof nylon

☐ GETTING UP

Hang-gliders are usually launched by jumping off the top of cliffs, hills or mountains.

Control bar

☐ STEERING A HANG-GLIDER

A hang-glider is steered by the control bar. Moving this bar alters the position of the pilot's bodyweight and the angle of the wings. Pushing the control bar out makes the hang-glider go up, for example.

CLIMBING

DIVING

TURNING

AILERONS, ELEVATORS & RUDDERS

All but the simplest aircraft have moveable parts on the wings and tail. These moveable parts are the ailerons, the elevators and the rudder. Together they are known as control surfaces, and they are used to change the direction of the flow of the air so that the aircraft can turn or tilt in flight. Two or three control surfaces have to be moved at once even to make a simple turn. The three main movements aircraft make are called rolling, pitching and yawing.

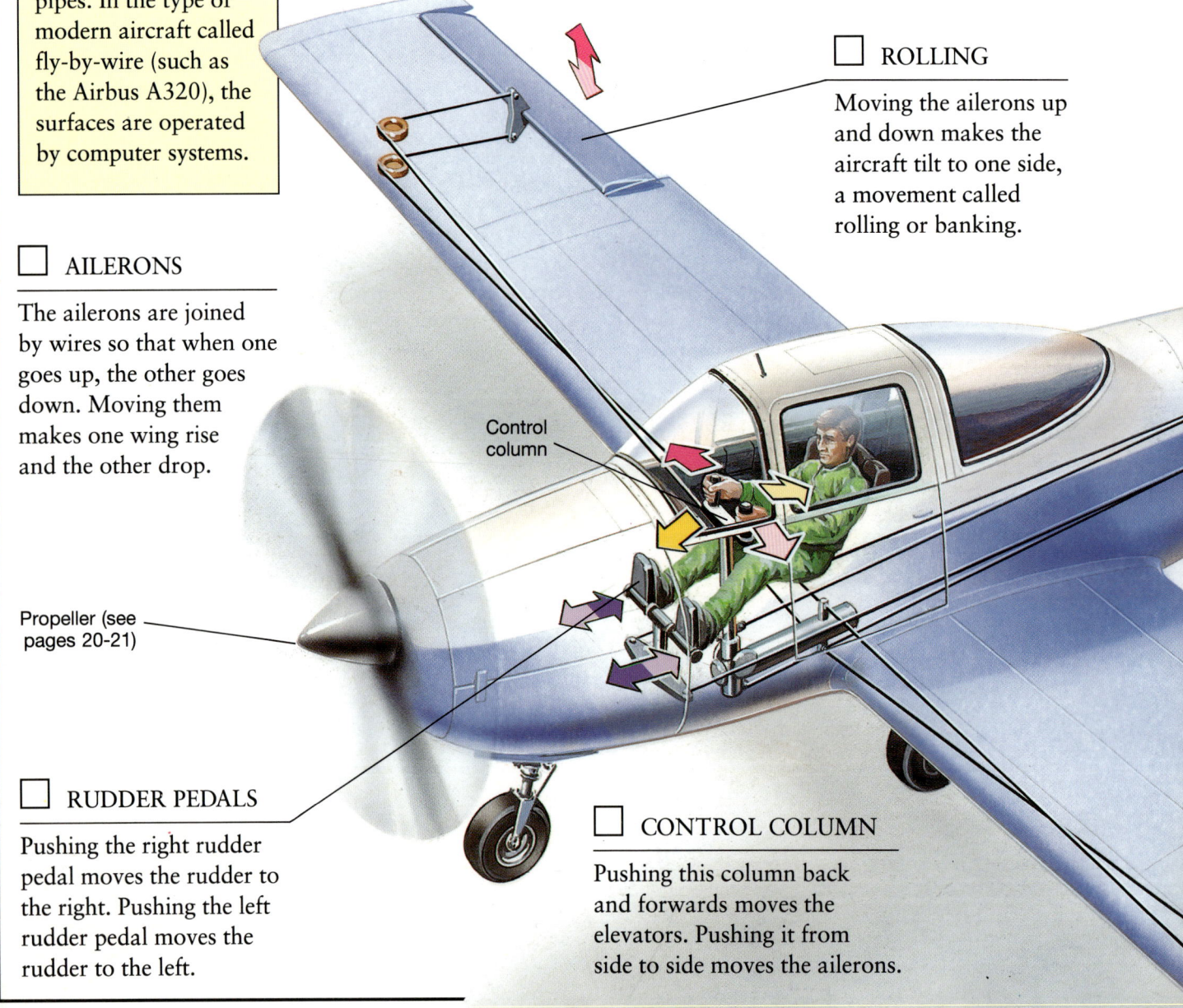

Control column

Propeller (see pages 20-21)

☐ AILERONS

The ailerons are joined by wires so that when one goes up, the other goes down. Moving them makes one wing rise and the other drop.

☐ ROLLING

Moving the ailerons up and down makes the aircraft tilt to one side, a movement called rolling or banking.

☐ RUDDER PEDALS

Pushing the right rudder pedal moves the rudder to the right. Pushing the left rudder pedal moves the rudder to the left.

☐ CONTROL COLUMN

Pushing this column back and forwards moves the elevators. Pushing it from side to side moves the ailerons.

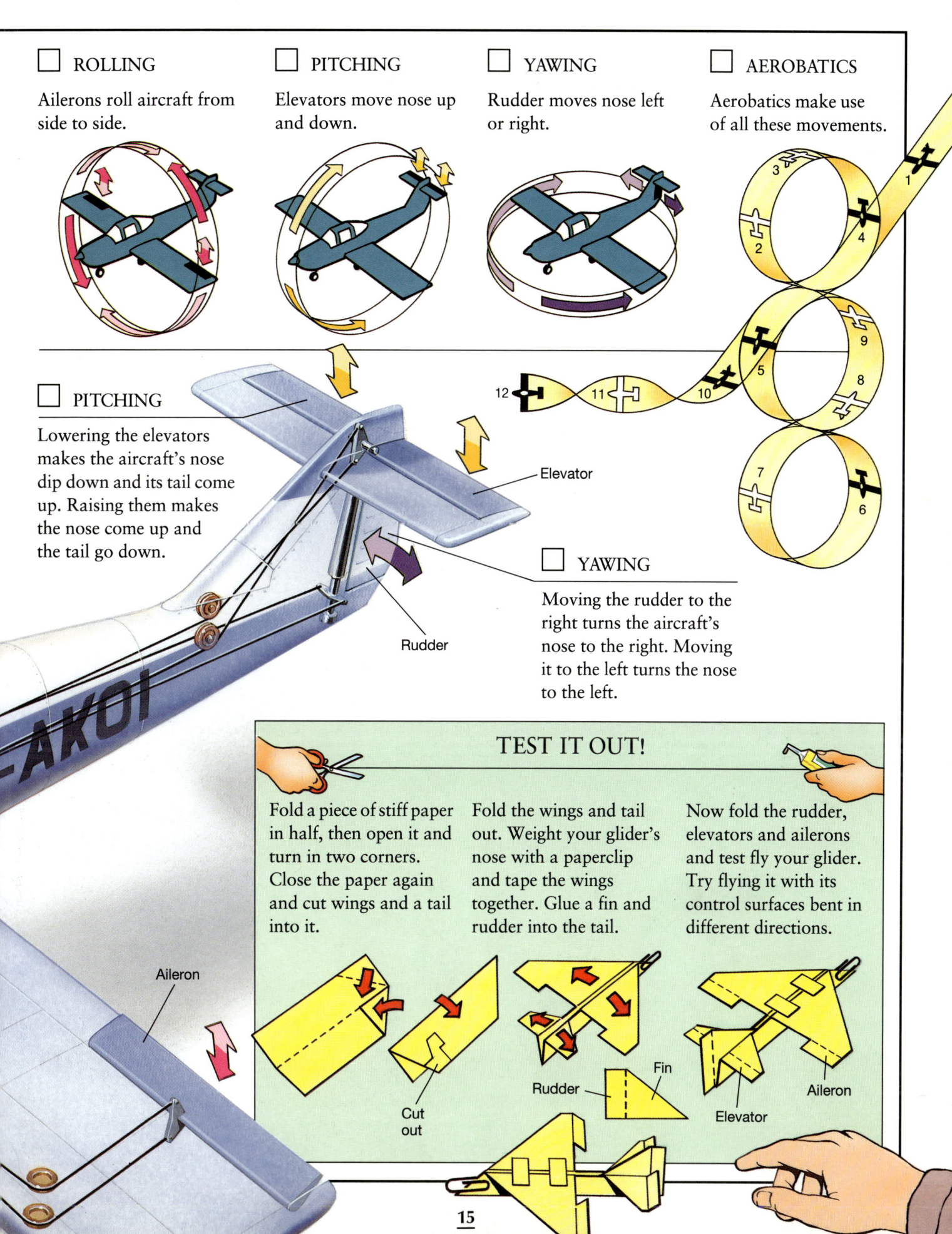

☐ ROLLING

Ailerons roll aircraft from side to side.

☐ PITCHING

Elevators move nose up and down.

☐ YAWING

Rudder moves nose left or right.

☐ AEROBATICS

Aerobatics make use of all these movements.

☐ PITCHING

Lowering the elevators makes the aircraft's nose dip down and its tail come up. Raising them makes the nose come up and the tail go down.

Elevator

Rudder

☐ YAWING

Moving the rudder to the right turns the aircraft's nose to the right. Moving it to the left turns the nose to the left.

Aileron

TEST IT OUT!

Fold a piece of stiff paper in half, then open it and turn in two corners. Close the paper again and cut wings and a tail into it.

Fold the wings and tail out. Weight your glider's nose with a paperclip and tape the wings together. Glue a fin and rudder into the tail.

Now fold the rudder, elevators and ailerons and test fly your glider. Try flying it with its control surfaces bent in different directions.

Cut out

Rudder

Fin

Elevator

Aileron

Streamlining cuts down drag or air resistance by helping air to flow smoothly past things. Objects that have a teardrop shape, such as wings and other aerofoils, are streamlined.

Teardrop shape, low drag

Square objects are not streamlined. They have sharply angled edges which break up the air flow, churning the air up behind the object and creating turbulence. This results in drag.

Square shape, high drag

THRUST, DRAG & STREAMLINING

Apart from gliders and hang-gliders, all aircraft are propelled forwards through the air by a jet engine or an engine-driven propeller. This forward-moving force is called thrust. However, air rubs against objects moving through it, slowing them down. This slowing force is called drag or air resistance. Engineers have discovered that there is less drag when things have a smooth streamlined shape.

1 WRIGHT *FLYER*, 1903

With its braced double wings, this famous aircraft had no streamlining at all. Even the pilot's body stuck into the air flow. But drag increases with speed, and early aircraft didn't fly fast enough to make streamlining really necessary.

Wingspan 12.29 m

Top speed 48 km/h

2 JUNKERS F13, 1919

Streamlining improved with the introduction of the single wing and the enclosed cockpit and cabin. The Junkers F13 was the first all-metal airliner in service.

Top speed – 140 km/h
Wingspan – 17.75 m

☐ FLIGHT FORCES

Four forces act on an aircraft in flight. An aircraft will fly only when the lift created by air flowing over its wings is greater than its weight, and when the thrust of its engines is greater than the drag of the air.

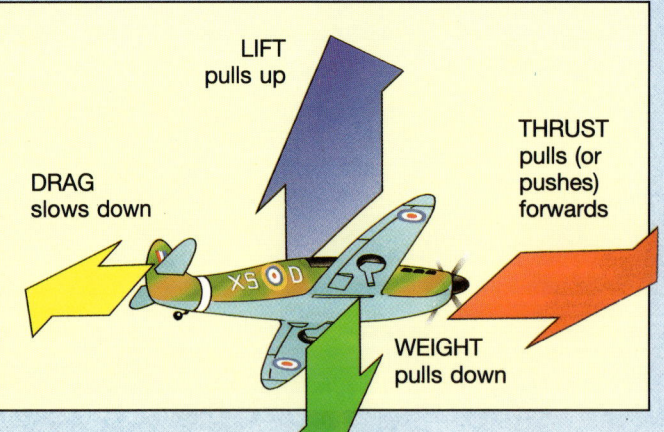

LIFT pulls up

DRAG slows down

THRUST pulls (or pushes) forwards

WEIGHT pulls down

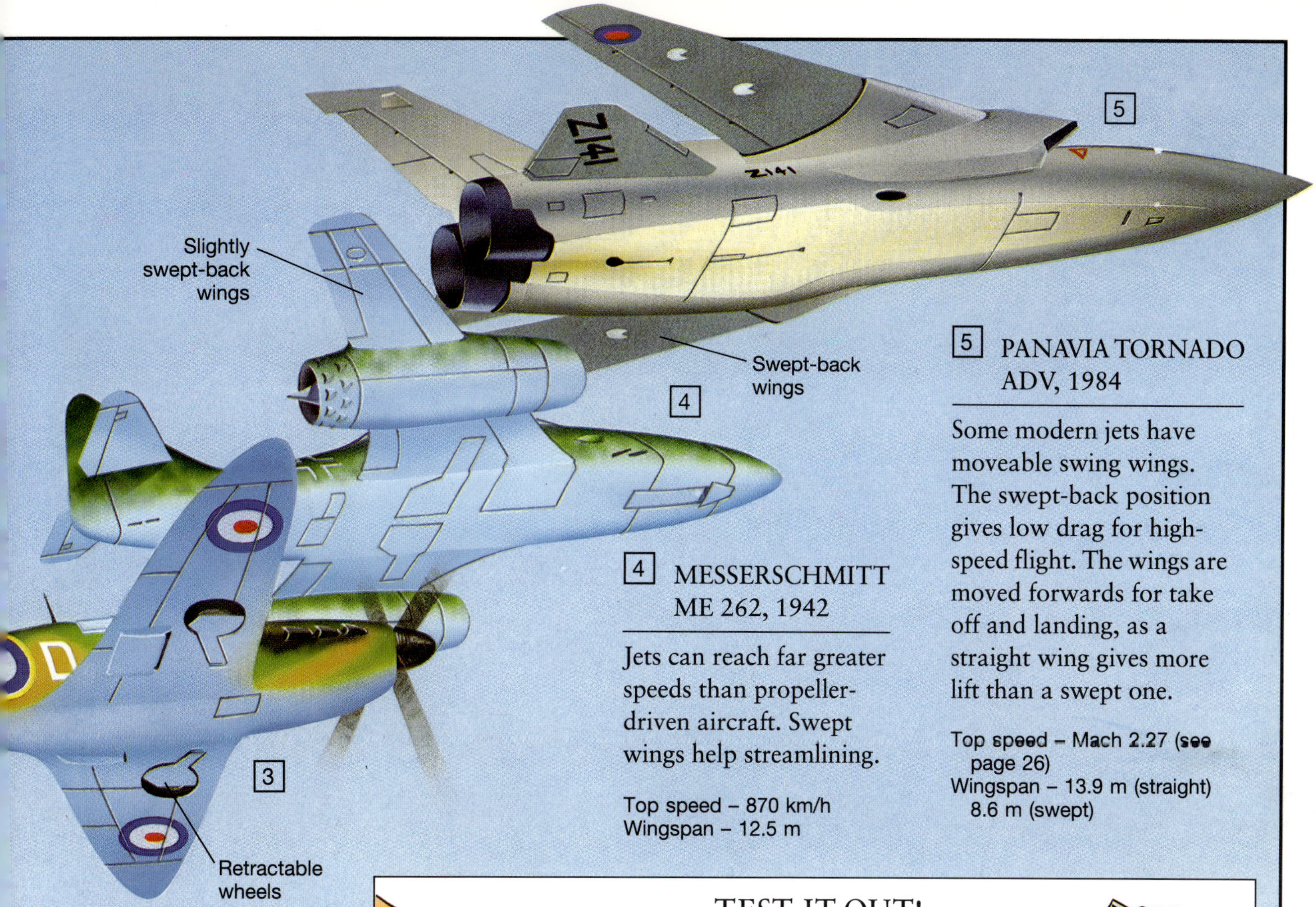

Slightly
swept-back
wings

Swept-back
wings

[4]

[5]

[5] PANAVIA TORNADO ADV, 1984

Some modern jets have
moveable swing wings.
The swept-back position
gives low drag for high-
speed flight. The wings are
moved forwards for take
off and landing, as a
straight wing gives more
lift than a swept one.

Top speed – Mach 2.27 (see
   page 26)
Wingspan – 13.9 m (straight)
   8.6 m (swept)

[4] MESSERSCHMITT ME 262, 1942

Jets can reach far greater
speeds than propeller-
driven aircraft. Swept
wings help streamlining.

Top speed – 870 km/h
Wingspan – 12.5 m

[3]

Retractable
wheels

[3] SUPERMARINE SPITFIRE, 1936

This was among the first
aircraft to have retract-
able main wheels – they
could be pulled up out of
the air flow, thus cutting
down drag and increasing
speed. During World War
II, the Spitfire became
famous as a combat
machine.

Top speed – 571 km/h
Wingspan – 11.23 m

TEST IT OUT!

This simple experiment
will show you how a
curved streamlined
shape helps air flow.
The piece of card you
use should be the same
height and width as the
metal can.

Stand about 30 cm away
and try to put the candle
out by blowing hard at the
card. You won't be able to
because the card breaks up
the flow of your breath
and prevents it from
reaching the flame.

Now replace the card
with the can, and try the
experiment again. The
candle will go out this
time, because your
breath flows round the
smooth curved sides of
the can.

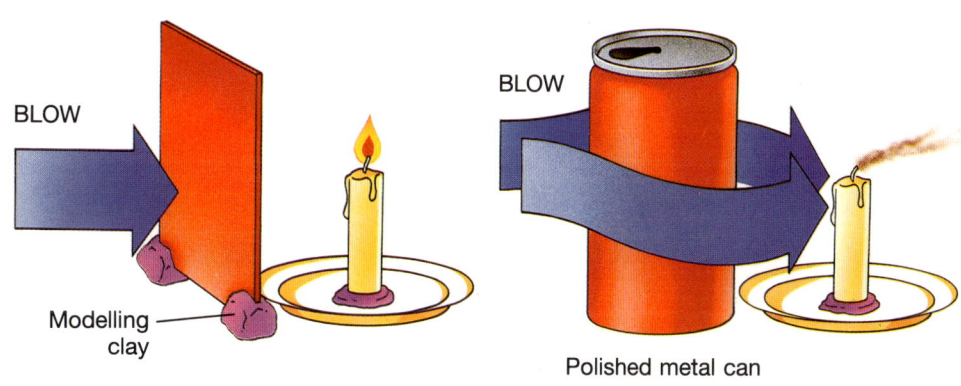

BLOW

Modelling
clay

BLOW

Polished metal can

FOCUS ON PARACHUTES

Parachutes have a great many uses, from making emergency escapes from damaged aircraft, to dropping soldiers and military vehicles in enemy countries, and dropping food and medical supplies to places where there are no roads or airfields. They are even used to help some types of high-speed vehicle such as dragsters to slow down and stop. Parachuting is also a popular sport.

As well as slowing aircraft down as they move forwards, drag or air resistance also slows falling objects. Parachutes are designed to use this effect. It is drag pushing against the large underside area of a parachute canopy that slows the fall of people or objects to give them a safe landing.

Drogue chute

Helmet

Spare parachute

Canopy

1 FREE-FALL

The parachutist free falls to about 600 metres above the ground, then pulls a ripcord to open the parachute pack.

2 DROGUE CHUTE

A small chute called a drogue opens first. It pulls out the main chute.

TEST IT OUT!

You can feel the effect of drag or air resistance for yourself if you run holding a large piece of board upright in front of you. The faster you run, the harder the air will push against the board, slowing you up.

Try running with the board held flat to your side. There is less drag, and running is easier.

3 MAIN CHUTE

Drag slows the parachutist's fall. In sports parachutes like the one shown here, air fills the canopy forming an aerofoil which can be flown rather like a hang-glider.

Steering lines

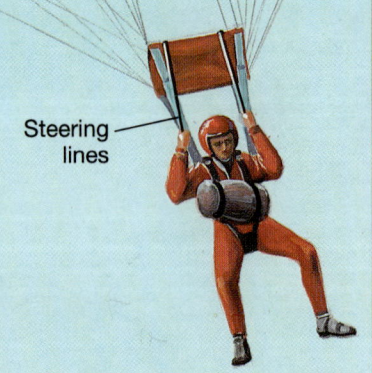

EJECTOR SEATS

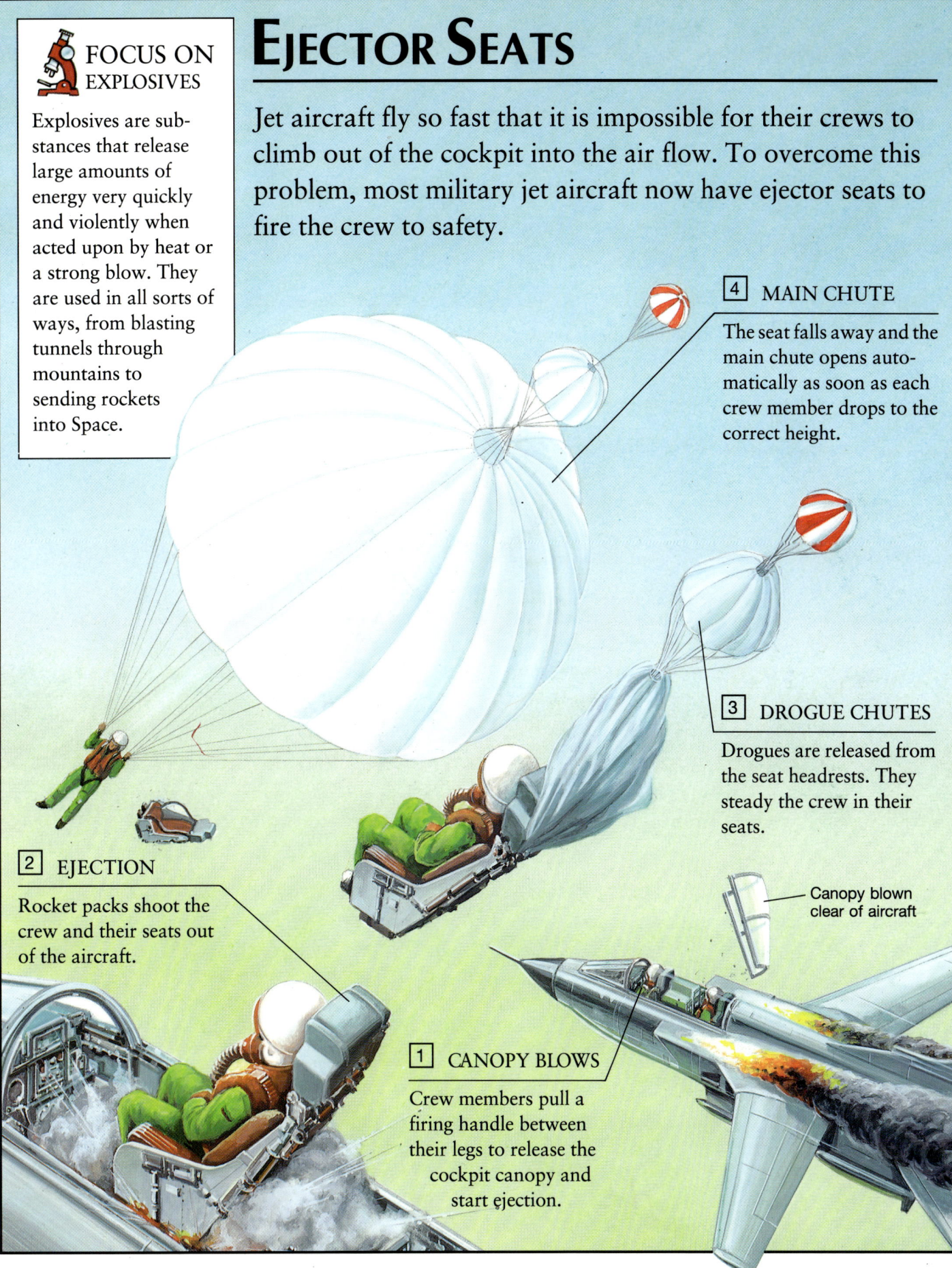

FOCUS ON EXPLOSIVES

Explosives are substances that release large amounts of energy very quickly and violently when acted upon by heat or a strong blow. They are used in all sorts of ways, from blasting tunnels through mountains to sending rockets into Space.

Jet aircraft fly so fast that it is impossible for their crews to climb out of the cockpit into the air flow. To overcome this problem, most military jet aircraft now have ejector seats to fire the crew to safety.

4 MAIN CHUTE

The seat falls away and the main chute opens automatically as soon as each crew member drops to the correct height.

3 DROGUE CHUTES

Drogues are released from the seat headrests. They steady the crew in their seats.

Canopy blown clear of aircraft

2 EJECTION

Rocket packs shoot the crew and their seats out of the aircraft.

1 CANOPY BLOWS

Crew members pull a firing handle between their legs to release the cockpit canopy and start ejection.

The first aircraft propellers were made from wood. But as faster aircraft were built, wood had to be replaced by stronger but heavier materials such as steel. The propellers on some modern aircraft include a material called carbon fibre, which is strong but very light.

PROPELLERS

Propellers are sometimes called airscrews because of the way they work. As an aircraft propeller turns, its blades pull air in from the front and push it out to the back. This propels the aircraft forwards, in much the same way as a screw being driven into a piece of wood. At the same time propeller blades also work rather like spinning wings, because they have an aerofoil shape. Instead of lifting upwards, however, they thrust the aircraft forwards. Propellers are driven by the aircraft's engines.

☐ PROPELLER TYPES

Propellers come in many types and sizes. The simplest has two blades. Some modern airliners have six-bladed propellers as these can give enough thrust while spinning fairly slowly and quietly.

Twin-blade   Three-blade   Four-blade   Six-blade

☐ PROPELLER MOUNTINGS

Propeller mountings also vary. The most common is either a single propeller on the nose or one propeller on each wing. The Cessna 336 Skymaster's front-and-back propeller arrangement is rare.

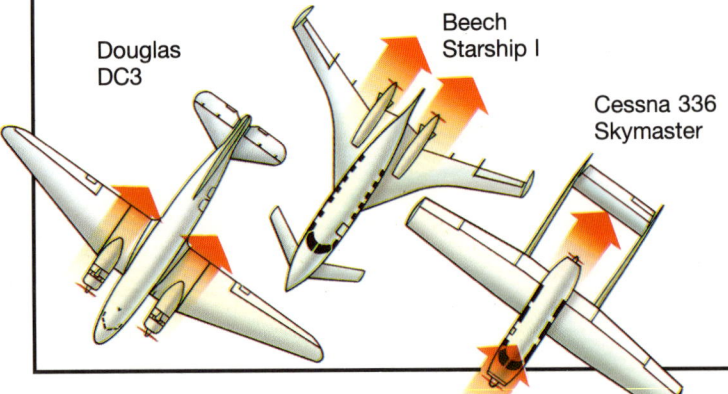

Douglas DC3

Beech Starship I

Cessna 336 Skymaster

TEST IT OUT!

You'll need to buy a small propeller and a piece of balsa wood from a model shop for this experiment.

Carefully push two pieces of stiff wire through the ends of the balsa wood, then bend the wire ends into hooks. Hang this on a piece of tightly stretched nylon line. Now thread the propeller, a bead, and a short piece of tube from a used ballpoint pen on to another piece of wire, bending the ends into hooks.

Stretch a rubber band between the two hooks, as shown below. Wind up the propeller a few times, then let it go. As the propeller spins, it will pull your balsa wood 'aircraft' along the nylon line.

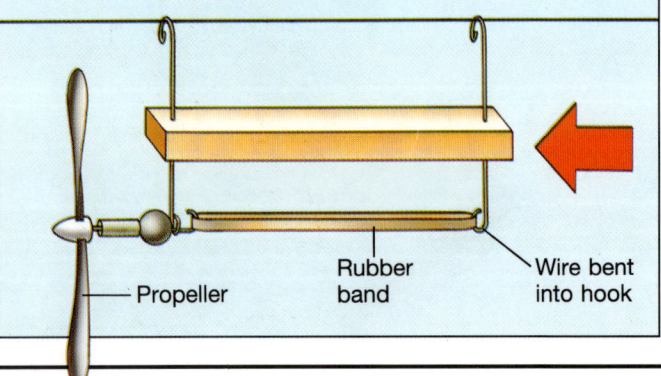

Propeller   Rubber band   Wire bent into hook

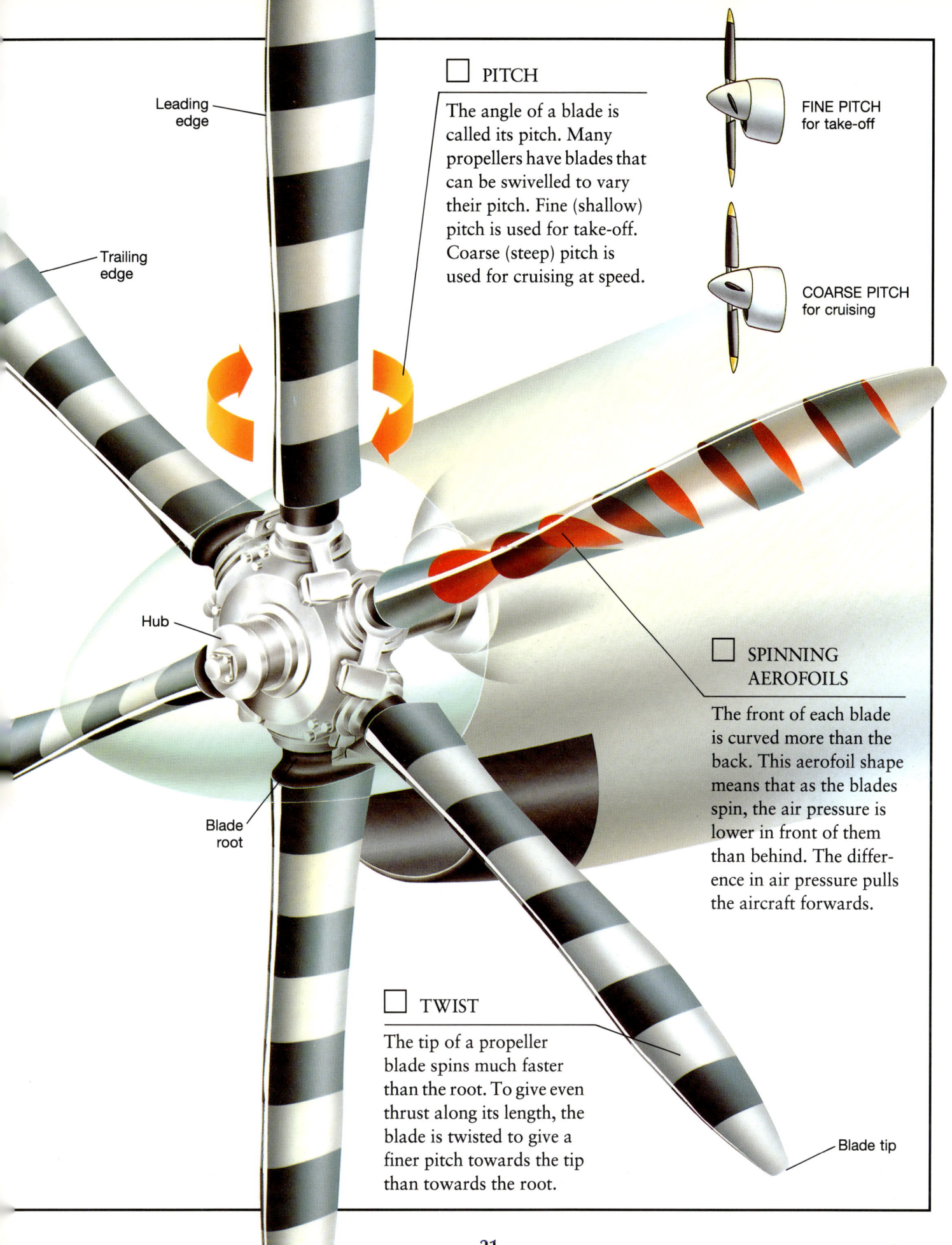

Leading edge

Trailing edge

□ PITCH

The angle of a blade is called its pitch. Many propellers have blades that can be swivelled to vary their pitch. Fine (shallow) pitch is used for take-off. Coarse (steep) pitch is used for cruising at speed.

FINE PITCH for take-off

COARSE PITCH for cruising

Hub

Blade root

□ SPINNING AEROFOILS

The front of each blade is curved more than the back. This aerofoil shape means that as the blades spin, the air pressure is lower in front of them than behind. The difference in air pressure pulls the aircraft forwards.

□ TWIST

The tip of a propeller blade spins much faster than the root. To give even thrust along its length, the blade is twisted to give a finer pitch towards the tip than towards the root.

Blade tip

If a helicopter's engines fail, the air that rushes through its rotor blades as it falls makes them spin, lowering the helicopter to safety.

Nature thought of this first, however! The fruits of trees such as sycamore, maple and ash are shaped rather like rotor blades. Instead of dropping straight to the ground when they fall from the tree, the fruits spin and are carried gently by the wind to new places to grow.

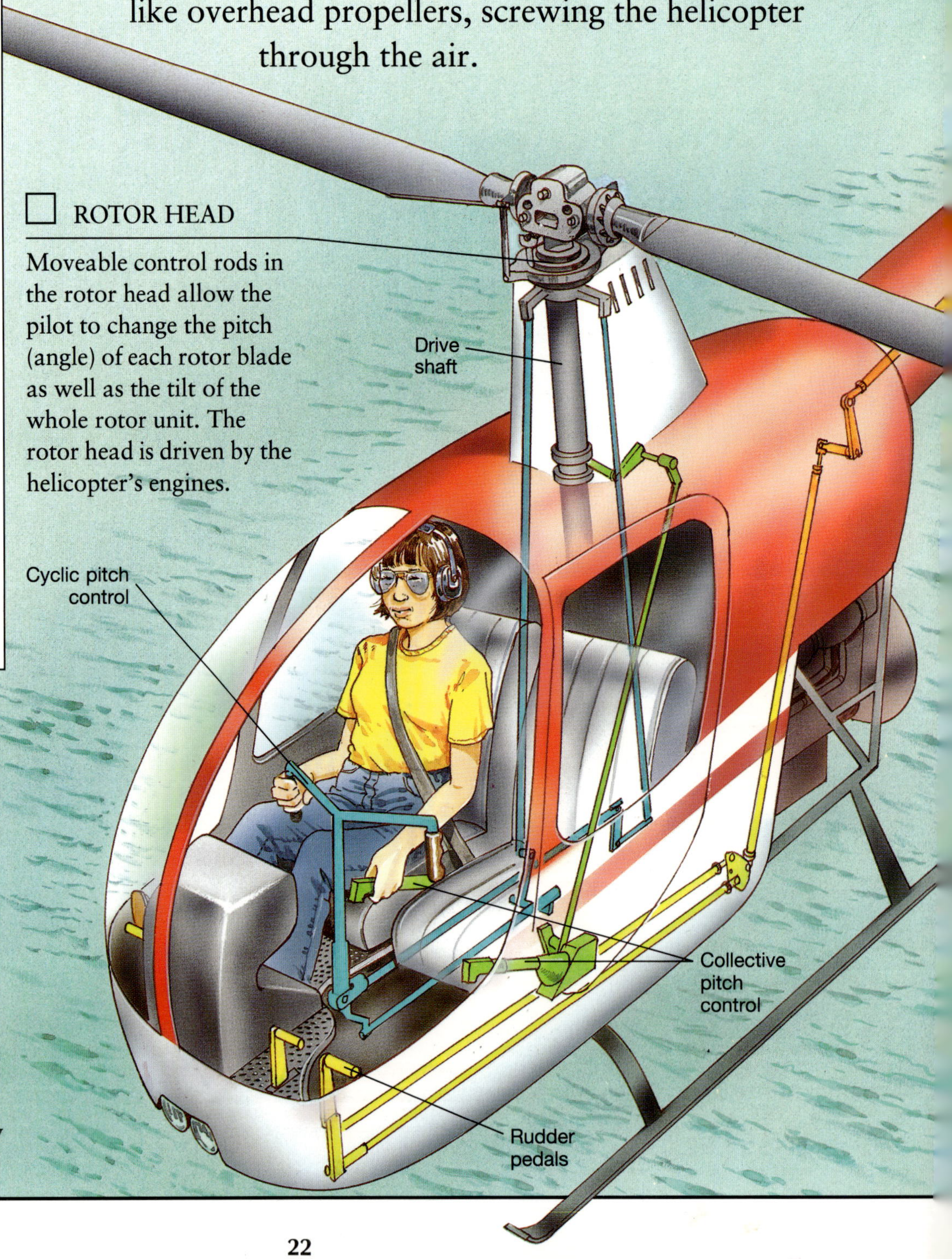

☐ CONTROLS

The pilot has three main controls. Rudder pedals alter the pitch of the tail rotor blades.

The cyclic pitch control tilts the main rotor unit forwards, backwards or sideways to direct the helicopter's flight.

The collective pitch control changes the pitch of the rotor blades to vary the amount of lift.

HELICOPTERS

Most aircraft can only fly forwards, but helicopters can fly backwards and forwards, as well as straight up or down – they can even hover on one spot. Helicopters can do all of this because they get both lift and thrust from their spinning rotor blades. These have an aerofoil shape and work rather like overhead propellers, screwing the helicopter through the air.

☐ ROTOR HEAD

Moveable control rods in the rotor head allow the pilot to change the pitch (angle) of each rotor blade as well as the tilt of the whole rotor unit. The rotor head is driven by the helicopter's engines.

Drive shaft

Cyclic pitch control

Collective pitch control

Rudder pedals

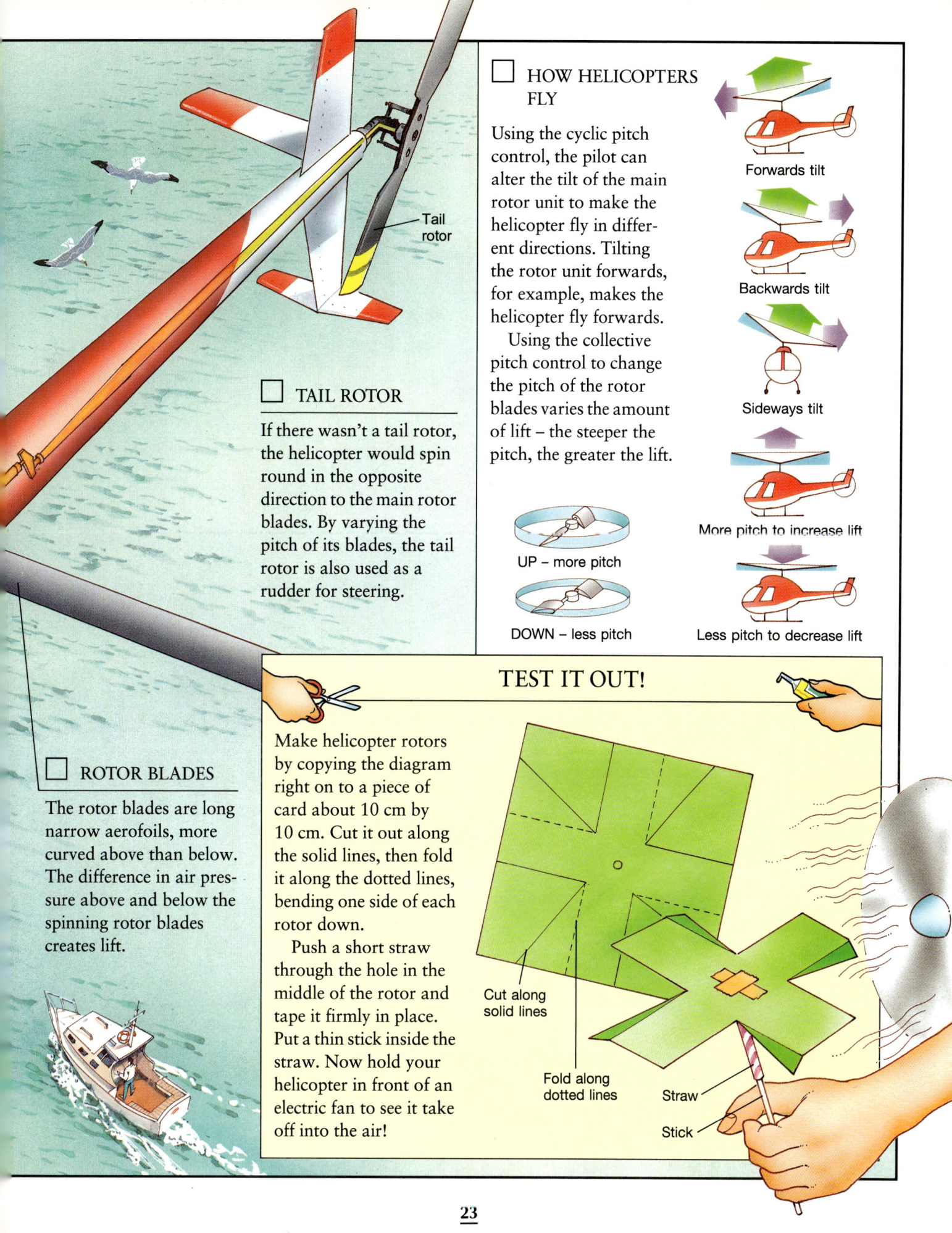

Tail
rotor

Using the cyclic pitch
control, the pilot can
alter the tilt of the main
rotor unit to make the
helicopter fly in differ-
ent directions. Tilting
the rotor unit forwards,
for example, makes the
helicopter fly forwards.

Using the collective
pitch control to change
the pitch of the rotor
blades varies the amount
of lift – the steeper the
pitch, the greater the lift.

Forwards tilt

Backwards tilt

Sideways tilt

More pitch to increase lift

Less pitch to decrease lift

UP – more pitch

DOWN – less pitch

☐ TAIL ROTOR

If there wasn't a tail rotor,
the helicopter would spin
round in the opposite
direction to the main rotor
blades. By varying the
pitch of its blades, the tail
rotor is also used as a
rudder for steering.

☐ ROTOR BLADES

The rotor blades are long
narrow aerofoils, more
curved above than below.
The difference in air pressure above and below the
spinning rotor blades
creates lift.

TEST IT OUT!

Make helicopter rotors
by copying the diagram
right on to a piece of
card about 10 cm by
10 cm. Cut it out along
the solid lines, then fold
it along the dotted lines,
bending one side of each
rotor down.

Push a short straw
through the hole in the
middle of the rotor and
tape it firmly in place.
Put a thin stick inside the
straw. Now hold your
helicopter in front of an
electric fan to see it take
off into the air!

Cut along
solid lines

Fold along
dotted lines

Straw

Stick

JET ENGINES

In his third law of motion (1687), the scientist Sir Isaac Newton stated that for every action there is an equal and opposite reaction.

Jet engines provide thrust because of action and reaction. The gases that rush out of the back of the engine (the action) thrust the aircraft in the opposite direction (the reaction).

All aircraft get thrust from engines – either piston engines, which work rather like car engines, or jet engines. Jet engines can propel aircraft to far greater speeds than piston engines, and nowadays almost all airliners, most military aircraft, and many small business aircraft are powered by them. There are three main types of jet engine – turbojet, turboprop and turbofan (main illustration).

Jet engines suck air in at one end and force it out of the other at a much greater speed. This thrusts the engine, and the aircraft, in the opposite direction.

1 FRONT FAN

This huge spinning fan at the front of the turbofan engine sucks air in. Some of the air goes into the compressor. But most is pushed straight around the engine, quietening it as well as creating thrust.

AIR IN

Engine casing

TEST IT OUT!

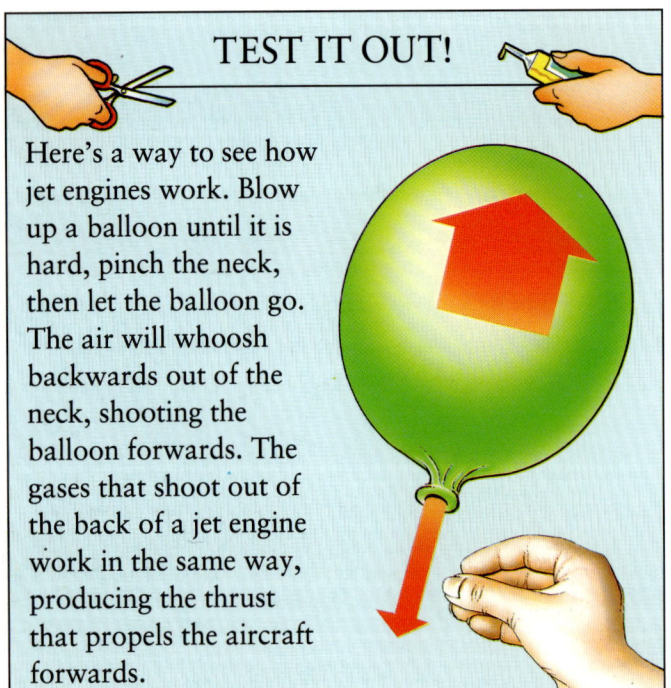

Here's a way to see how jet engines work. Blow up a balloon until it is hard, pinch the neck, then let the balloon go. The air will whoosh backwards out of the neck, shooting the balloon forwards. The gases that shoot out of the back of a jet engine work in the same way, producing the thrust that propels the aircraft forwards.

2 COMPRESSOR

The air is compressed (squashed together) inside here, so that as much as possible is forced into the combustion chamber.

TURBOJET ENGINES

Turbojets are an earlier type of jet engine than turbofans, and they are noisier and use more fuel.

The supersonic airliner Concorde is one of the few passenger aircraft that is still powered by turbojets.

TURBOPROP ENGINES

These work like turbojets, but their turbines also drive a propeller which produces most of the

thrust. Turboprops use less fuel, but they are slower than either turbojets or turbofans.

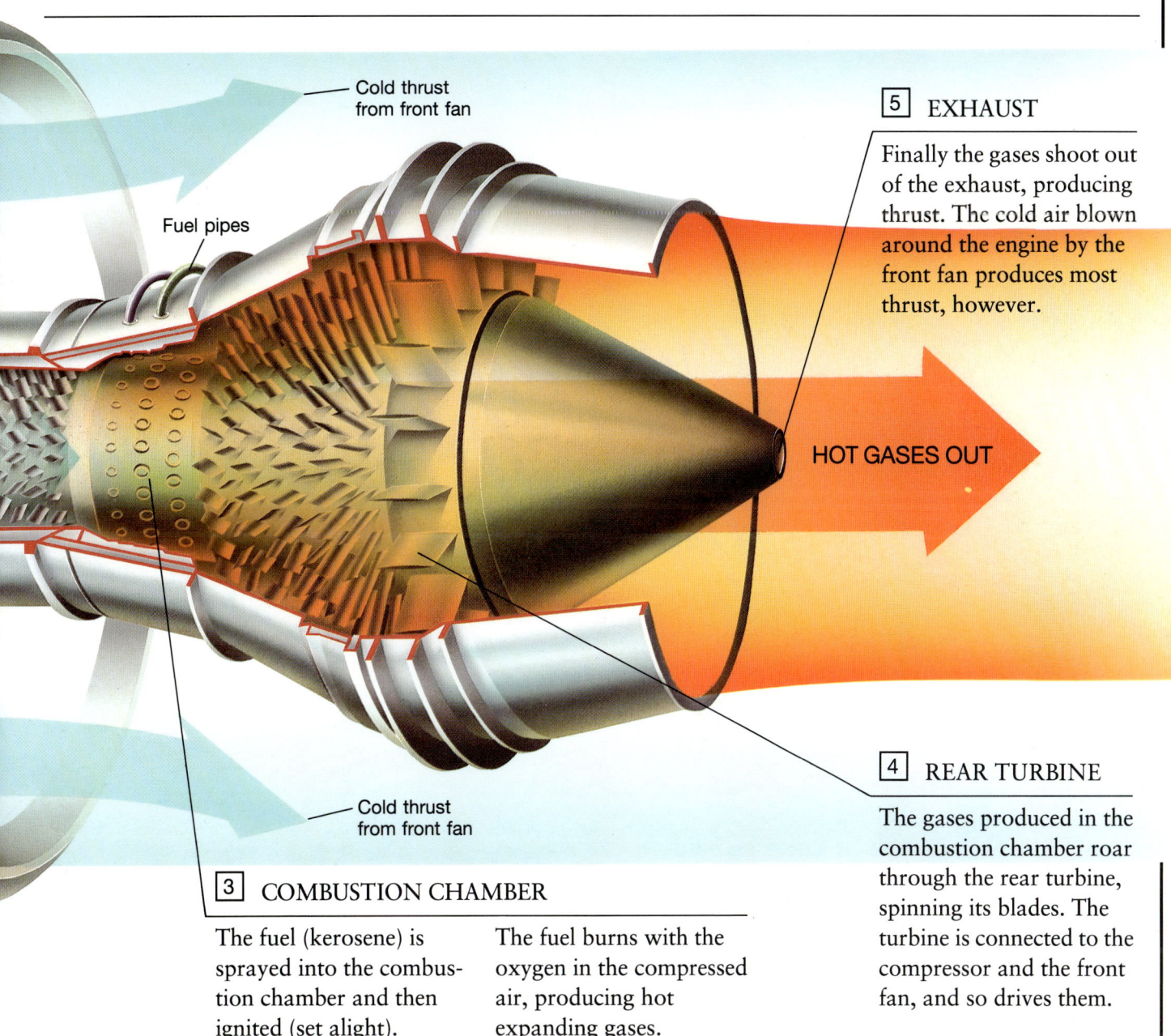

Compressor   Combustion   Turbine

AIR IN

Compressor   Combustion   Turbine

AIR IN

Cold thrust from front fan

Fuel pipes

Cold thrust from front fan

5 EXHAUST

Finally the gases shoot out of the exhaust, producing thrust. The cold air blown around the engine by the front fan produces most thrust, however.

HOT GASES OUT

4 REAR TURBINE

The gases produced in the combustion chamber roar through the rear turbine, spinning its blades. The turbine is connected to the compressor and the front fan, and so drives them.

3 COMBUSTION CHAMBER

The fuel (kerosene) is sprayed into the combustion chamber and then ignited (set alight).

The fuel burns with the oxygen in the compressed air, producing hot expanding gases.

FOCUS ON MACH NO.

This measurement of speed is named after the man who worked it out, the Austrian scientist Ernst Mach (1838-1916).

Dividing an aircraft's speed by the speed of sound gives you the Mach number. For example, Mach 1 is the speed of sound (about 1060 km/h at 11,000 metres), Mach 2 is twice the speed of sound, and so on.

Supersonic flight is faster than the speed at which sound travels. The speed of sound is around 1225 km/h at sea level, then it slowly drops with height. Above about 11,000 metres it stays the same, about 1060 km/h.

When aircraft fly faster than the speed of sound, the air in front of them becomes compressed (squashed) and forms a shock wave. This travels right down to Earth where we hear it as a loud bang called a sonic boom.

1 BELL X-1

In 1947, Chuck Yeager piloted this US rocket-powered aircraft to Mach 1.015. It was the first aircraft to fly faster than the speed of sound in level flight.

Wingspan 8.53 m

Rocket engine

TEST IT OUT!

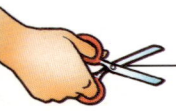

Sound is energy made when something vibrates (moves backwards and forwards). Sonic booms are so loud that they can make vibrations that are strong enough to break or damage windows and even buildings.

See how sound waves vibrate. Put a little sugar on some plastic film stretched over a jar. Hold something metal about 10 cm away from the jar and bang it hard. The sugar will bounce as the bang makes the film vibrate.

2 NORTH AMERICAN F100 SUPER SABRE

This was the first jet-powered aircraft to exceed the speed of sound in level flight. In 1953 it reached Mach 1.17.

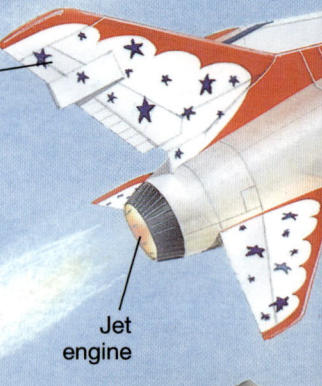

Jet engine

3 AÉROSPATIALE CONCORDE

Powered by four turbojet engines, the Anglo-French Concorde can cruise at Mach 2.2. It first flew in 1969.

Wingspan 25.6 m

Turbojet engines

4 LOCKHEED SR-71 BLACKBIRD

This US spy aircraft reached Mach 3.3 in 1976. It is still the world's fastest jet aircraft today. Although SR-71s are no longer in military service, some are now being used for scientific studies into the upper atmosphere.

Wingspan 16.94 m

Wingspan 11.82 m

5 NORTH AMERICAN X-15

The fastest aircraft are powered by rockets, and the world record holder is the X-15. In 1967, it reached Mach 6.72.

Wingspan 6.7 m

☐ BREAKING THE SOUND BARRIER

As an aircraft flies, waves of air pressure (shown below as rings) form around it. These pressure waves move ahead of the aircraft because they travel at the speed of sound.

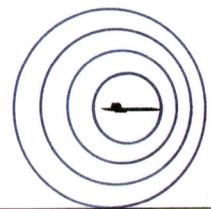

As the aircraft nears the speed of sound, it catches up with the pressure waves. They bunch up into a shock wave, which travels out on either side of the aircraft's flight path.

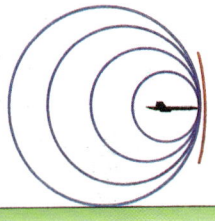

As the aircraft accelerates beyond the speed of sound, it breaks through the shock wave. The shock wave angles back behind the aircraft, reaching the ground as a sonic boom.

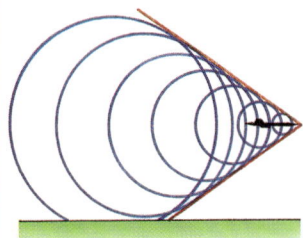

INSIDE A JET AIRLINER

Although modern jumbo jets such as the Boeing 747-400 cruise at less than half the speed of the supersonic airliner Concorde, they use roughly the same amount of fuel to carry four times as many passengers. Airliners like the 747 are very large and very heavy, of course. They are also among the most complex machines ever built, consisting of over 4.5 million separate parts.

□ BOEING 747-400

The 747-400 is 70.4 metres long with a wing-span of 65.15 metres. Fully loaded, it weighs nearly 406 tonnes. This airliner can carry more than 400 passengers and crew, plus up to 13 tonnes of cargo, a distance of 12,700 km without refuelling.

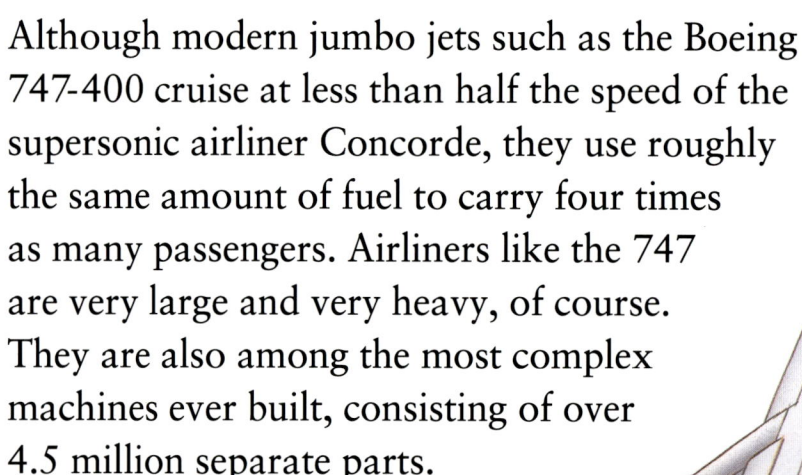

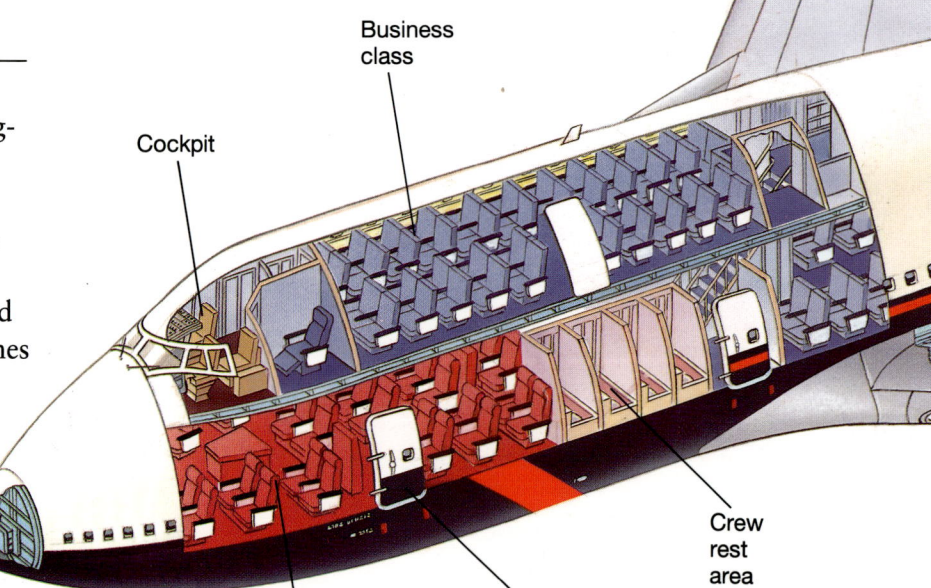

Cockpit

Business class

Weather radar (see page 34)

First class

Front exit

Crew rest area

□ ENGINE MOUNTINGS

Jet airliners show great variety in the number and position of their engines. All airliners are designed so that they are able to land safely on just one engine, if the others fail.

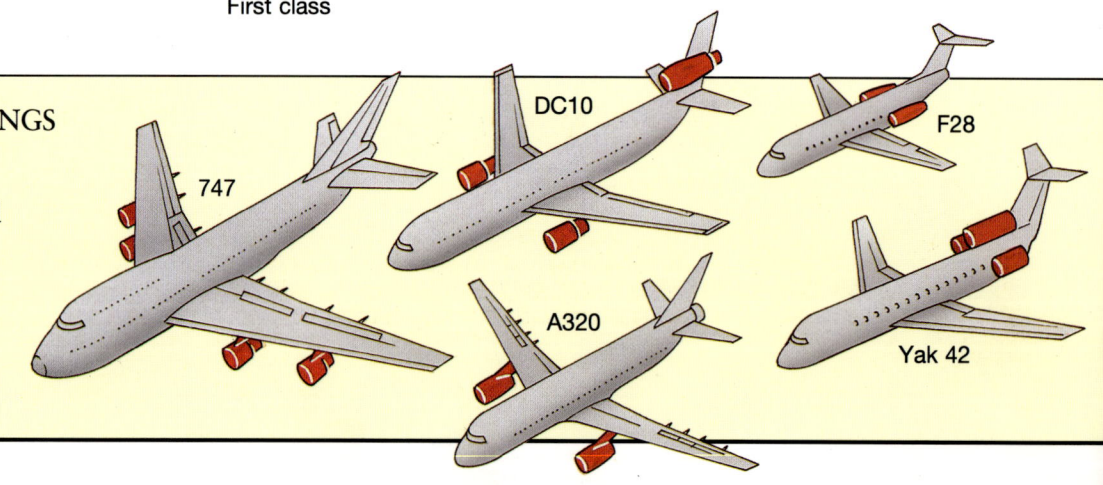

747

DC10

F28

A320

Yak 42

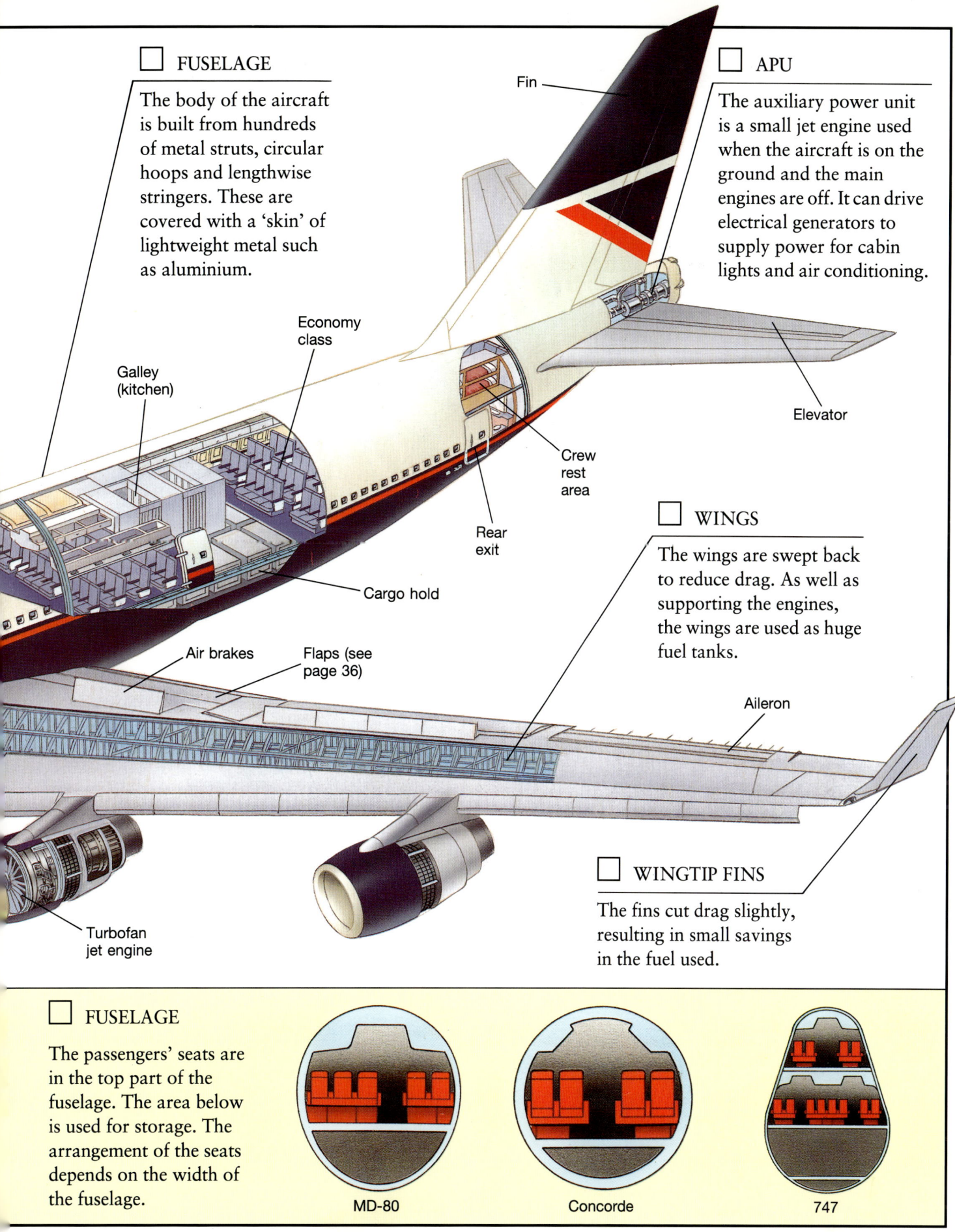

FUSELAGE

The body of the aircraft is built from hundreds of metal struts, circular hoops and lengthwise stringers. These are covered with a 'skin' of lightweight metal such as aluminium.

Fin

APU

The auxiliary power unit is a small jet engine used when the aircraft is on the ground and the main engines are off. It can drive electrical generators to supply power for cabin lights and air conditioning.

Economy class

Galley (kitchen)

Crew rest area

Elevator

Rear exit

Cargo hold

WINGS

The wings are swept back to reduce drag. As well as supporting the engines, the wings are used as huge fuel tanks.

Air brakes

Flaps (see page 36)

Aileron

WINGTIP FINS

The fins cut drag slightly, resulting in small savings in the fuel used.

Turbofan jet engine

FUSELAGE

The passengers' seats are in the top part of the fuselage. The area below is used for storage. The arrangement of the seats depends on the width of the fuselage.

MD-80

Concorde

747

ON THE FLIGHT DECK

The flight deck is the airliner's nerve centre. It is from here that the captain and the co-pilot control all the instruments and systems that keep the airliner flying safely on course. Until recently the flight deck was a mass of mechanical dials, gauges and switches. These are now being replaced with electronic instruments and computer screens.

FOCUS ON AUTOPILOT

Modern airliners are so complicated that computers are used to help pilots to fly them. Frequent computer checks are run during the flight to ensure that all the airliner's systems are working properly. The auto-pilot is a computer used on long flights to fly the airliner auto-matically. The pilots simply keep an eye on it to check that the flight is going according to plan.

☐ FLIGHT CREW

Only two flight crew – the captain and the co-pilot – are needed at the controls of most modern airliners. Many of the systems that in the past were managed by a third crew member, the flight engineer, are now monitored by electronic equipment.

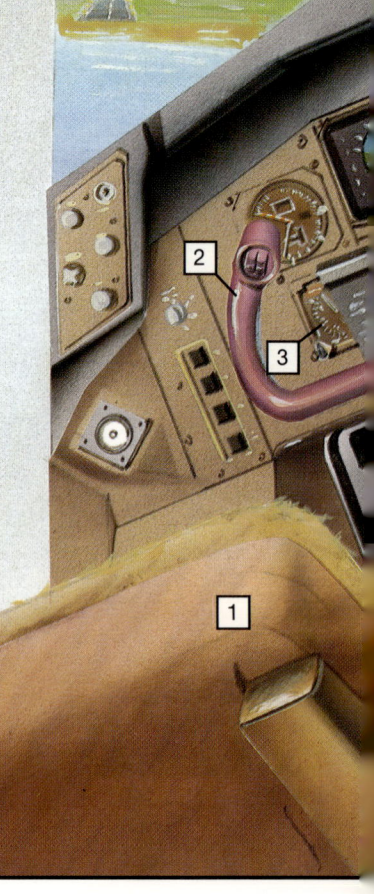

☐ ASI

The air speed indicator (no. 7 in the main illus-tration) shows speed in knots (1 knot is equal to 1.85 km/h) and Mach number. Information about the aircraft's speed through the air is fed to the ASI from a sensor called the pitot tube, which is outside the aircraft.

☐ ALTIMETER

This instrument (no. 15) shows height above sea level by measuring the air pressure outside the aircraft. Air pressure decreases with height, so the lower the air pressure, the higher the aircraft is. The altimeter measures height above sea level in feet.

☐ EADI

The electronic attitude director indicator (no. 6) tells the captain whether the aircraft is flying level. The T-bars are the air-craft, and the line between blue and green marks the horizon. When banking, the horizon tilts to match the angle of the ground as seen from the cockpit.

BOEING 767 COCKPIT

1 Captain's seat	5 Standby magnetic compass	9 Engine systems display	13 Engine fire detection and shut-off controls
2 Control column	6 EADI	10 Engine thrust levers	14 Flaps lever
3 Radio compass	7 Air speed indicator	11 Parking brake handle	15 Altimeter
4 Engine ignition	8 Landing gear lever	12 VHF radio	16 Rudder pedals

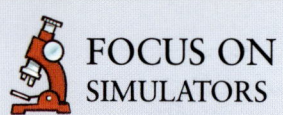

Flight simulators
allow the pilots of
military aircraft to
practise their battle
skills in safety.

FLIGHT SIMULATOR

Flight simulators are rather like giant computer games. They are not toys, though. They are used to train pilots to fly new types of aircraft and to practise general flying skills, including what to do in emergencies. It is safer to practise on the ground than in the air and, as real aircraft don't have to be flown, flight simulators also save on fuel costs.

☐ FLIGHT DECK

Each simulator has the same flight deck as a particular type of aircraft, with all the usual controls. An instructor sits behind the pilots.

☐ PROJECTORS

Scenes of real airports around the world are made by computers and projected on to a screen outside the cockpit window. This lets pilots practise taking off and landing in all conditions. Aircraft sounds are fed through loudspeakers inside the simulator.

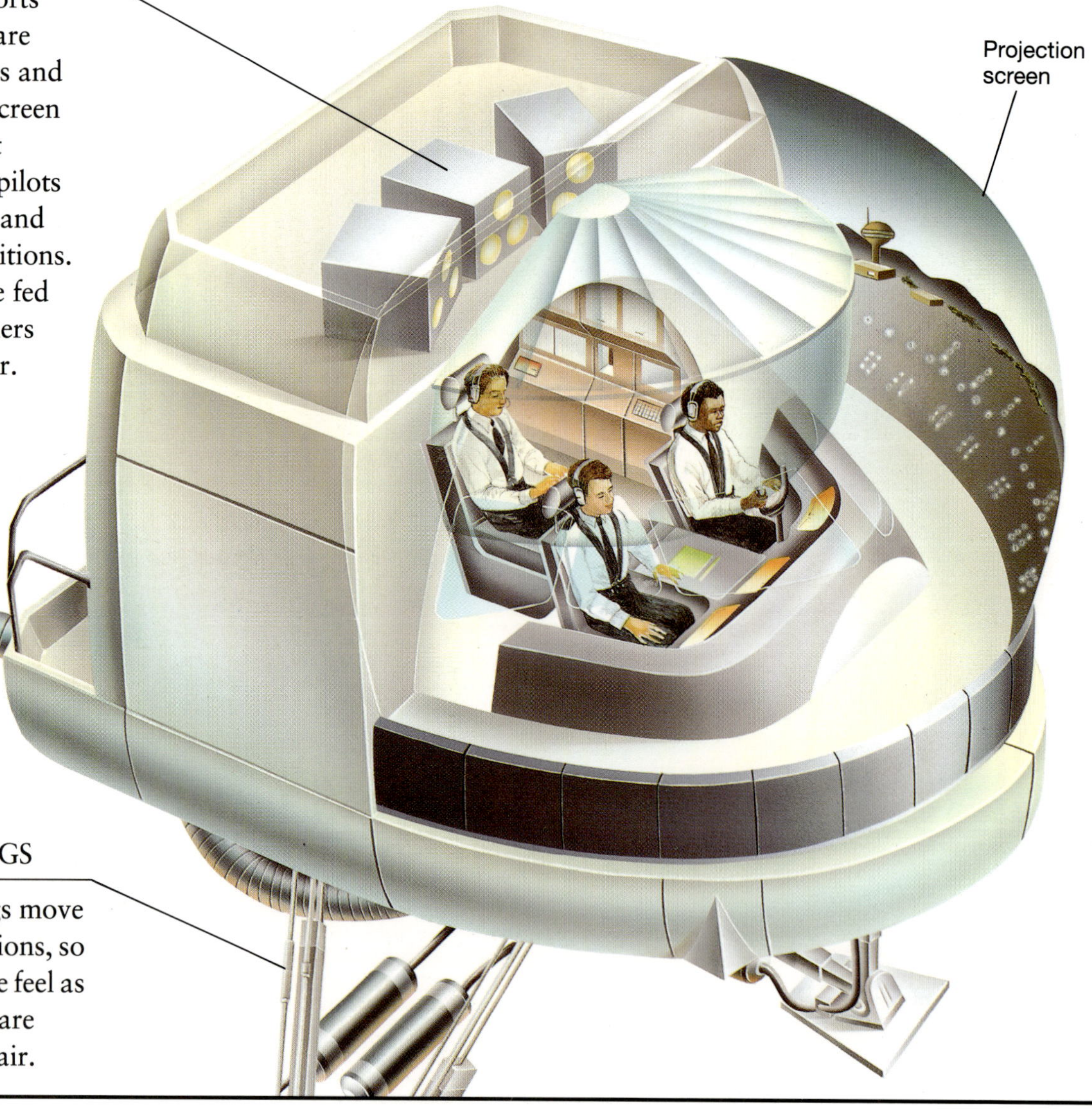

Projection screen

Electricity cable

☐ MOVING LEGS

The simulator's legs move to tilt it in all directions, so that the pilots inside feel as though they really are flying through the air.

AIR SAFETY

Flying is one of the safest ways to travel. Every part of an airliner is regularly checked to make sure it is working properly, and every stage of a flight is carefully controlled. In the rare event that something does go wrong, the crew help passengers to get out of the aircraft quickly and safely.

FOCUS ON BLACK BOX

Although it is often called a black box, the fire- and crash-proof flight data recorder is usually red!

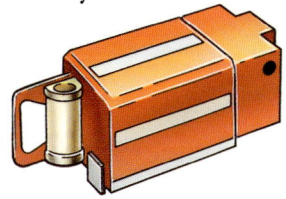

Instruments inside it record everything that happens to the air-craft's main systems, and even what the flight crew are saying to each other. If there is an accident, this information helps investigators to work out why it happened and how to stop it happening again.

☐ LIFE JACKETS

These are stored under the seats in case of emergency landings at sea. When passengers are outside the aircraft, they pull a toggle to make their jackets fill with air.

☐ ESCAPE CHUTES

In emergency landings, chutes are inflated at exits. At sea, the chutes may be used as life rafts. On land, people slide down them to the ground.

☐ LIFE JACKETS

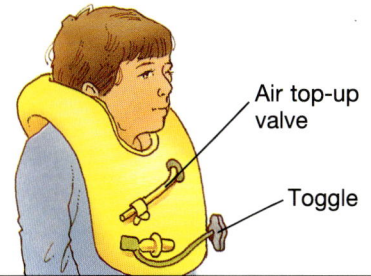

Air top-up valve

Toggle

☐ OXYGEN MASKS

Air pressure decreases with height above ground, so the cabin is pressurized (with air at normal ground-level pressure). If the cabin air pressure falls, oxygen masks drop to allow people to breathe safely.

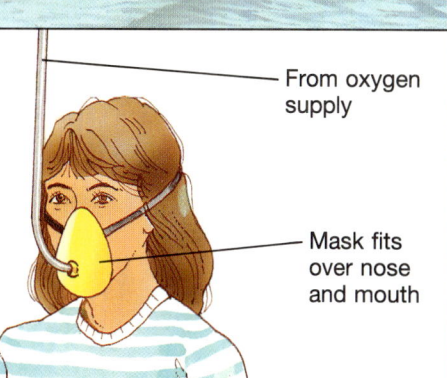

From oxygen supply

Mask fits over nose and mouth

Most airliners have radar equipment in their nose cones which tells them if there is bad weather ahead, or objects such as other aircraft which they might fly into.

The word radar is short for RAdio Detection And Ranging. Radar works by sending out short bursts of radio signals.

Like echoes, these radio signals bounce off any object they hit, including clouds. The aircraft's computers work out how far away the object is from the time the signals take to bounce back. Radio signals would take 1/500th of a second to return from an object 300 km away, for example.

The information picked up by the radar equipment is displayed on a screen on the airliner's flight deck.

FINDING THE WAY

Fast modern aircraft such as airliners fly so high that pilots cannot navigate (find their way) by watching the ground – they are usually high above the clouds and cannot see the ground at all. So pilots and air traffic controllers have electronic systems to help them navigate. These systems use information beamed from radio equipment on the aircraft, on the ground, and on satellites orbiting high above the Earth.

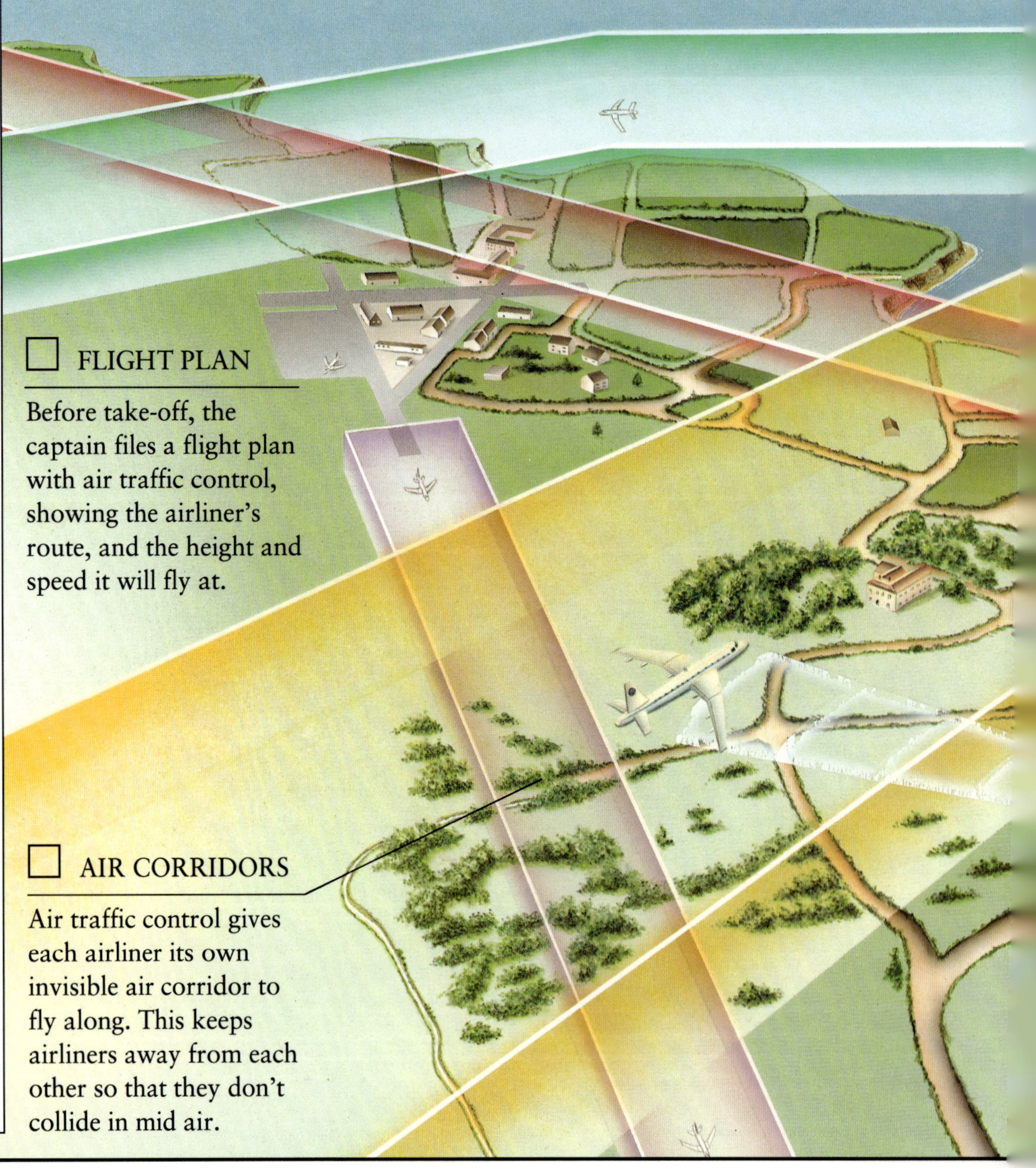

☐ FLIGHT PLAN

Before take-off, the captain files a flight plan with air traffic control, showing the airliner's route, and the height and speed it will fly at.

☐ AIR CORRIDORS

Air traffic control gives each airliner its own invisible air corridor to fly along. This keeps airliners away from each other so that they don't collide in mid air.

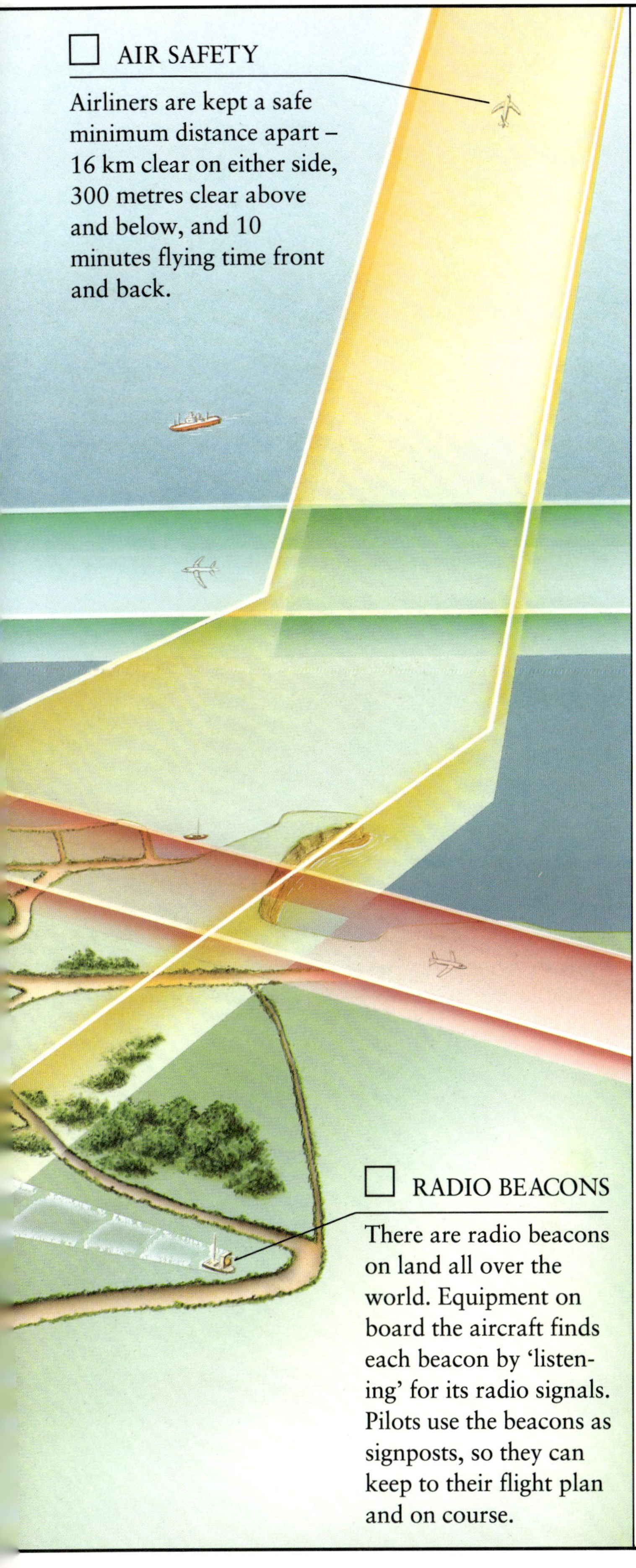

☐ AIR SAFETY

Airliners are kept a safe minimum distance apart – 16 km clear on either side, 300 metres clear above and below, and 10 minutes flying time front and back.

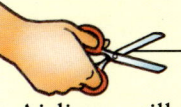

☐ RADIO BEACONS

There are radio beacons on land all over the world. Equipment on board the aircraft finds each beacon by 'listening' for its radio signals. Pilots use the beacons as signposts, so they can keep to their flight plan and on course.

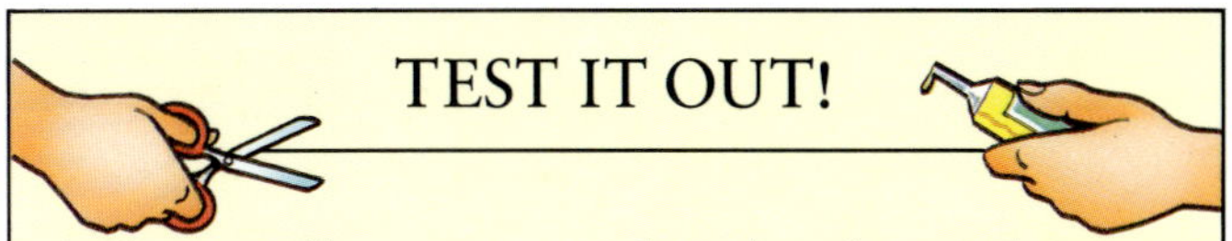

TEST IT OUT!

Airliners still carry a standby magnetic compass just in case their electronic systems fail (see page 31, no. 5).

Magnetize a large sewing needle by using the same end of a magnet to stroke it gently along its whole length at least 20 times. Now float a 1-cm-thick slice of cork in a bowl of water. Lay the magnetized needle on top of the cork. The needle will swing round so that it points North-South, just like the needle of a real magnetic compass.

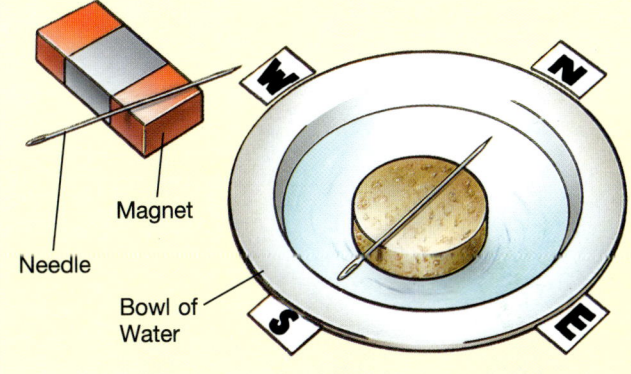

Needle

Magnet

Bowl of Water

☐ AIR TRAFFIC CONTROL

In the area around and above an airport, each aircraft is guided by air traffic controllers who speak to the captain by radio. Information about each aircraft's height and position is collected by radar antennae at the airport and shown on radar screens in the control tower.

1 CLEARED FOR TAKE-OFF

When permission to take off comes, the airliner taxis on to the runway. The captain opens the throttle but keeps the wheel brakes on. The engines scream as they build up power.

TAKING OFF

Before an airliner can take off, the flight crew have to check that its instruments and systems are working properly. Then, when the airliner is ready to leave, the captain radios the control tower for permission to start the engines and taxi into position next to the start of the runway. The airliner waits there for permission to take off.

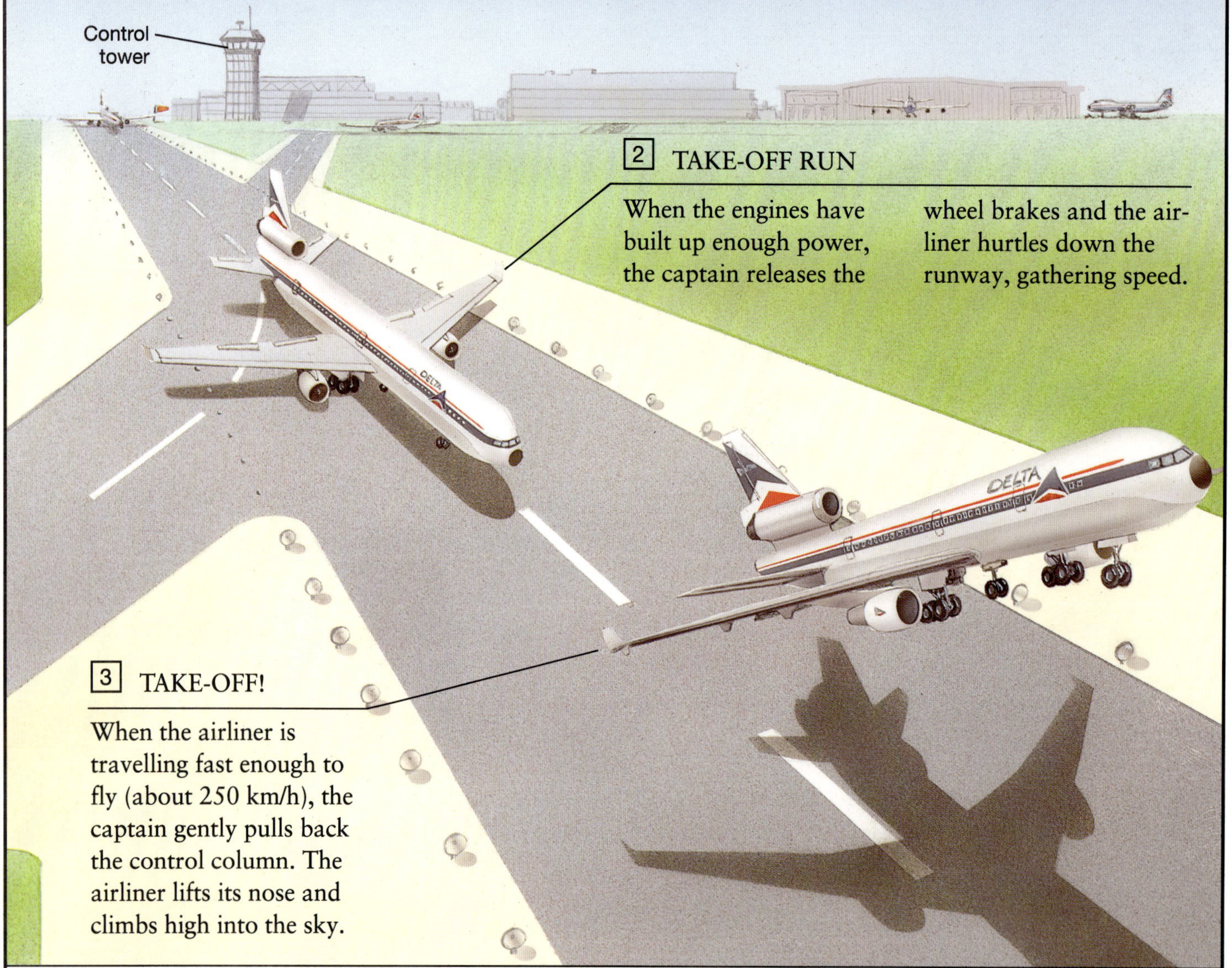

Control tower

2 TAKE-OFF RUN

When the engines have built up enough power, the captain releases the wheel brakes and the airliner hurtles down the runway, gathering speed.

3 TAKE-OFF!

When the airliner is travelling fast enough to fly (about 250 km/h), the captain gently pulls back the control column. The airliner lifts its nose and climbs high into the sky.

☐ FLAPS

Most large aircraft have extra moveable parts called flaps (see pages 28-29) on their wings. These are used to produce extra lift with low drag at take-off, and extra lift with extra drag when landing.

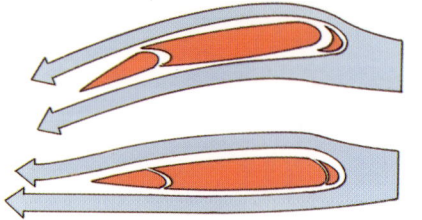

TAKE-OFF
Extra lift with low drag

NORMAL FLIGHT

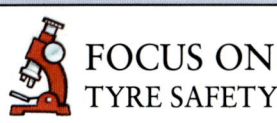
COMING IN TO LAND

When an airliner nears the airport at the end of its flight, the captain radios air traffic control to ask for permission to land. The controllers then talk to the flight crew by radio to help them fly the airliner safely towards the runway. The captain cuts the engine power back to make the airliner lose speed and height as it comes in to land.

2 TOUCHDOWN

As soon as the airliner is on the ground, the captain usually puts the engines into reverse thrust and applies the wheel brakes to slow the aircraft down.

1 APPROACH

As the airliner nears the runway, the captain flares (raises) the nose. This allows the main wheels to touch the ground first to take up the shock of landing.

REVERSE THRUST

Reverse thrust can be used to help slow a jet aircraft down, once it has landed safely on the runway.

Metal sections fold out of the engines, to direct the jet blast forwards so that it acts as a brake.

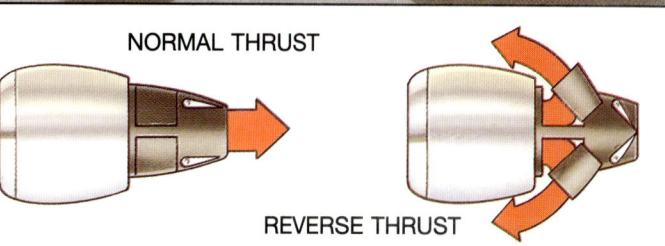

NORMAL THRUST

REVERSE THRUST

Vertical flight

Horizontal flight

VSTOL AIRCRAFT

Most modern aircraft need a fairly long runway to allow them time to reach take-off speed. Airliners like the 747 need a runway about 1500 metres long, for example. However, a few special types of aircraft are designed to use a very short runway or even no runway at all. They are known as VSTOL, which stands for Vertical or Short Take-Off and Landing.

The most successful VSTOL aircraft are the helicopter and the British Aerospace Harrier, which is often nicknamed the jump jet.

☐ WINGTIP WHEELS

These wheels balance the Harrier when it is on the ground. They fold up out of the air flow into the wing during normal flight.

☐ HARRIER – JUMP JET

The Harrier can fly up or down, sideways and backwards – it can even hover like a helicopter.

It is very useful as a fighter aircraft because it can take off and land almost anywhere.

TEST IT OUT!

The next time you have a bath, you can feel how the downward thrust of exhaust from its nozzles pushes the Harrier up into the air!

Hold the bath shower head so it points down, a few centimetres above the bottom of the bathtub. Then turn the cold water tap on very fast.

The cold water will gush out of the shower head with such force that it will push your hand and the shower head upwards!

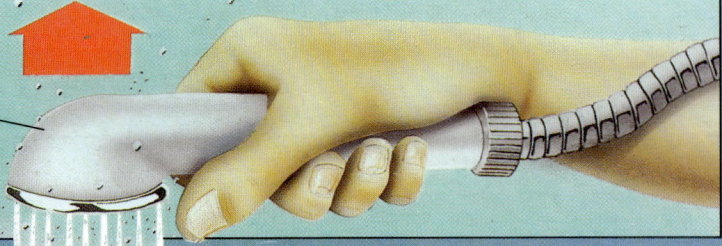

Shower head is thrust up by water power

☐ IN FLIGHT

The Harrier's wingspan is 7.7 metres. Its top speed at sea level is 1170 km/h (but 1050 km/h when fully loaded).

☐ SWIVELLING NOZZLES

The four exhaust nozzles have angled plates which can be swivelled to alter the direction of the exhaust gases from the engine, and therefore the thrust that propels the Harrier through the air. The nozzles can be moved from fully back, right round to pointing down.

Fully back for normal flight

Nozzle

Midway when accelerating or slowing down

Straight down for vertical flight and hoverng

Exhaust nozzle

Extra fuel tank

☐ ENGINE

The Harrier is powered by a single turbofan jet engine with four exhaust nozzles, two on either side of the fuselage.

☐ TAKING OFF

Vertical take-off uses more fuel than short take-off and is difficult when the Harrier is fully loaded. Because of this, the

Harrier usually makes a short take-off run. Some aircraft carriers have ski-jump ramps to help with short take-off.

INDEX

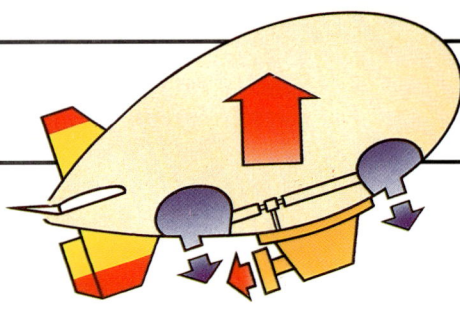
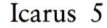

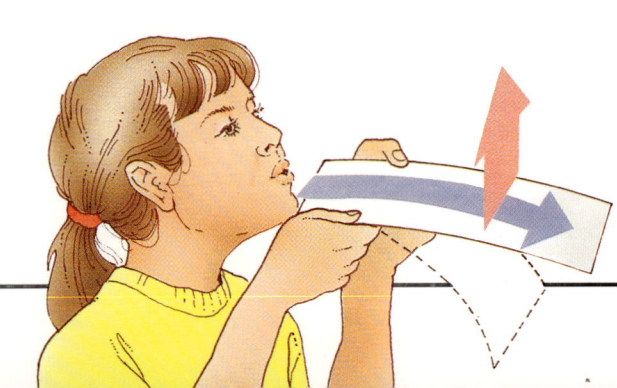